HIGHLY PAID EXPERT

Turn Your Passion, Skills, and Talents Into a Lucrative Career by Becoming the Go-To Authority in Your Industry

DEBBIE ALLEN
The Expert of Experts

Pompto

D0451580

THE HIGHLY PAID EXPERT
EDITED AND TYPESET BY KARA KUMPEL
Cover design by Rob Johnson
Printed in the U.S.A.

To order this title, please call toll-free 1-800-CAREER-1 (NJ and Canada: 201-848-0310) to order using VISA or MasterCard, or for fur-ther infor-mation on books from Career Press.

CAREER
PRESS
The Career Press, Inc.
220 West Parkway, Unit 12
Pompton Plains, NJ 07444
www.careerpress.com

Library of Congress Cataloging-in-Publication Data

Allen, Debbie, 1953–
    The highly paid expert : turn your passion, skills, and talents into a lucrative career by becoming the go-to authority in your industry / Debbie Allen.
        pages cm
    Includes index.
    ISBN 978-1-60163-321-7 (paperback) -- ISBN 978-1-60163-442-9 (ebook)
    1. Selling. 2. Strategic planning. 3. Customer relations. I. Title.
    HF5438.25.A4393 2014
    001--dc23
                                                                    2014008083

Disclaimer

The publisher and the author make no representations or warranties with respect to the accuracy or completeness of the contents of this work and specifically disclaim all warranties, including, without limitation, warranties of fitness for a particular purpose. No warranty may be created or suitable for every situation. This work is sold with the understanding that the publisher is not engaged in rendering legal, accounting, or other professional services. If professional assistance is required, the services of a competent professional person should be sought. Neither the publisher nor the author shall be liable for damages arising here-from. The fact that an organization or Website is referred to in this work as a referred source of further information does not mean that the author or the publisher endorses the information the organization or Website may provide or recommendations it may make. Further, readers should be aware that Internet Websites listed in this work may have changed or disappeared between when this work was written and when it was read.

This book is dedicated to the many mentors and experts who have molded my life-long career as an entrepreneur.

ACKNOWLEDGMENTS

Many people have helped me grow both personally and professionally, allowing me to succeed in just about any business I set my mind to. Without them, I would not be living such a joyful life doing what I love and having such a lucrative career that supports others.

Working with dozens of experts for more than 30 years has been like receiving a master's degree in business many times over. These experts have allowed me to confidently play a much bigger game by expanding my knowledge, intuition, creativity, and enthusiasm for business growth.

Their guidance ignited my passion for helping others expand their knowledge to become top experts and authorities in their chosen industries.

Working with my brilliant book agent, Jessica Faust of BookEnds, has helped me become a bestselling author and expand my knowledge to the masses. I couldn't imagine working with an agent who is more supportive, honest, and easy to work with. Thanks, Jessica!

Finally, I am deeply grateful to all of my wonderful clients, seminar attendees, support staff, and joint venture partners. Thank you for trusting me as your mentor, your teacher, your leader, and your friend.

CONTENTS

PREFACE

THERE HAS NEVER BEEN A BETTER TIME TO launch yourself as an expert. The Internet, social media, video marketing, and the print-on-demand industry have made it easier than ever before. There is still plenty of room online for you to dominate your marketplace, and I'm going to show you the way. In the pages of this book, I will reveal the hidden truth behind the expert industry, and I'll show you how to thrive as an expert.

Take this book seriously, because I'm going to give you the tools to quickly move miles beyond your competition by using my proven expert model. Read it word for word, page by page, with a highlighter in hand, because you'll want to pay close attention to all that is revealed. I've been teaching my expert model and developing highly paid thought leaders for years—but only to those clients who have paid me top dollar for my personalized mentoring. Now it's time for me to reveal those same strategies that took me years to perfect...with you. You are about to uncover the actual system I've used to develop highly successful experts in dozens of different niche markets.

For years, many so-called experts have tried to launch into this business and have failed. Many failed due to lack of knowledge of how to penetrate and dominate their market, whereas others launched with poor marketing plans that didn't allow them to stand out from their competitors. Even more failed due to a lack of direction and unfocused goals. It's one thing to have the passion, skill, or talent to inspire others, but it's another to make that inspiration pay the bills. Growing a lucrative career as an expert takes a well-thought-out business plan and a blueprint to follow.

The expert industry, for the most part, has been shrouded in mystery for far too long. This book uncovers secrets no other author or expert has dared to share before. You are about to discover why the expert industry is growing so rapidly and how you can jump onboard now to leave your impact on the world and create a lucrative career as a highly paid expert. My goal is to create more real experts than ever beforen so that they can help change lives with their wisdom, skills, and talents in support of others—all while prospering from a career they love.

Get ready to step up to a much bigger game in business and in life.

INTRODUCTION

PULLING BACK THE CURTAIN

IT'S TIME TO PULL BACK THE CURTAIN AND LOOK behind the scenes at the field of the highly paid expert. What's behind the curtain is an exciting opportunity for you to step up to a much bigger game in business and in life.

First, what is an expert? An expert is a known specialist who offers wisdom and solutions in the form of personal knowledge, skill, and/or guidance. What sets an expert apart from others who offer a service is that they specialize in a specific topic or niche market. They often offer their expertise in a formulated system or step-by-step program to allow their clients to gain fast results.

As you pull back the curtain (or pages of this book), you begin to imagine and visualize that you are already there: You are a well-known authority in your niche market. You are highly respected and highly paid for your expertise. You have ideal clients who greatly value your advice and are open to paying you top dollar for your opinions, experience, and knowledge. You live a life of supporting others, yet you are generously gifted with unlimited abundance. The world is paying attention to what you have to say. Opportunity and success flow to you easily, and you're living the life you have dreamed of. You've turned your passion, skills, and talents into a lucrative career as a highly paid expert.

It's all here waiting for you.

For the most part, the expert industry has been a mystery. Just a few years ago, we only thought of experts as Hollywood celebrities, celebrity speakers, wealthy entrepreneurs, and best-selling authors. We believed the expert industry was limited to a very small percentage of people. But that's no longer the case. The expert industry is now becoming more mainstream, and it's time for you to jump into this lucrative career with both feet.

I'm excited you have decided to take this journey along with me. There's no better time than right now for you to become the go-to expert in your niche market. Today, we are all searching for a better, faster, more effective way of doing things. The Internet has made it possible for us to instantly connect with experts on just about any topic in a matter of minutes. We can easily find advice on just about any topic at the touch of our fingertips. You may be thinking, *If it's that easy to find free information online, why would someone want to pay me top dollar for my information or listen to my advice?* The answer is, the Internet can only scratch the surface of the amount of information and guidance *you* can provide. Anyone who is serious about wanting to learn more about something will want to find the expert who can educate them in more depth.

Experts offer detailed how-to information that solves problems, offers solutions, and personally supports the success of others. Experts may communicate their knowledge with informational products sold on- and off-line, such as audio, video, books, and/or a system that promises a proven outcome or result. Or, they may communicate their expertise by speaking on teleseminars, Webinars, video, speaking engagements, and so on. They may also communicate with their clients by offering personalized coaching or consulting.

There are many ways for an expert to communicate, but the main goal is always the same: support others with your knowledge by helping them find solutions to their problems, and guide them to a more successful personal or professional life. If supporting others with your advice and getting paid well for it sounds like something that you are passionate about, the expert business is for you.

The World Needs Experts in Every Industry

As an entrepreneur, my background in business started at a very young age, but I had no formal training on how to become an expert. I built and sold numerous successful companies, and then one day I felt something was missing. That "something" was giving back to others. I had been blessed with many wonderful mentors in my life and believed it was time for me to begin supporting and mentoring others in return. At the time, I had no idea that I was going to become an expert. Times are different today; you can actually learn how to create expert status. It doesn't matter where you come from, what your background is, or what level of expertise you currently possess. My clients are in diverse industries. They are coaches, speakers, authors, accountants, doctors, engineers, and carpet cleaners. Some are already considered experts in their industry, and others are just beginning their careers. It doesn't matter what kind of business you focus on, because the world needs experts in every market.

What is so great about being the expert is that while you are fulfilling your own life's mission, you are also teaching others in return. As the expert, you go deeper with your knowledge than the average person in your industry and develop a step-by-step blueprint, program, or system that can be duplicated.

There is so much room and so much opportunity available to you now. The expert business is ripe for the picking and is ready to explode. The expert trend is one of the fastest-growing industries because people want information fast. They want the go-to expert, an authority on the information they need. They may want to quickly overcome an obstacle, discover solutions to a problem, get more clients, make more money, improve their sales, or just enjoy an improved quality of life. More people are looking for fast solutions to their problems, and they want the best experts in the business to show them the way.

Find Your Niche

Begin by finding a niche in a very specific market or industry. For example, don't decide to be a coach for women. That's too general and too broad. Focus more on a specific niche such as women executives in career transition.

For example, after building and selling successful retail clothing stores for more than 15 years, I launched my speaking and consulting business for retailers. My target market was focused only on my niche industry of retail. I always had a love for business and, most specifically, marketing. Therefore, my expertise was as a retail marketing authority. At first, I focused my marketing efforts to a specific group only—retail clothing and the gift industry. That was a big enough market to keep me busy while I grew my expertise as a speaker and consultant. I felt comfortable sharing my success stories and experience in this specific niche market. At the time, I had no idea I was also building a lucrative career as a professional speaker.

As my business and expertise grew, I expanded my retail marketing niche to other areas within the retail industry. The same marketing principles applied to all groups. At first, I wanted to stay close to what I knew from my own personal experience in order to launch myself into this new business as an expert. Yet, as I become more comfortable and was getting hired more, I began to expand my niche market.

When I started out my career as a speaker and retail consultant, I just wanted to give back to the industry, to help others. That was my main goal. I had been extremely fortunate to have had amazing mentors early on in my retail career. Before I had any experience in retail, I bought a losing business, and those mentors helped me grow the business into a multi-million-dollar company within a few short years. I knew that someday I wanted to give back and support the success of others who were growing their business too.

When I began speaking as my way of giving back, I was not particularly fond of it. But there was something inside of me when I was growing up that wanted a stage. I remember telling my mom that I wanted to be a singer. She laughed and said, "You can't sing." Now you might think that was a mean thing for her to say, but really, she was right! I switched my career choice and decided to become a dancer. But soon after that I realized that the only dancers who were making big money (especially in Indiana) had a pole to dance around. I changed my mind on that career move too.

The only way to get good at anything is to keep doing it. So that's exactly what I did with my speaking career. I wasn't a very good speaker at first, but people kept asking me back. They started paying me well because I had something to share that would help others cut their learning curve and succeed quickly. Audience members began asking me for personalized support, so it was easy to get consulting work without much effort. Next I self-published a book called *Trade Secrets of Retail Stars* to help build my credibility.

Being Financially Free Gives You Choices

Highly paid experts are in a position to choose because they understand that the most valuable asset they have to offer is their time. It's a great feeling when you are making good money and getting plenty of opportunity, and you can easily say yes or no to the opportunities that come your way. The financially free expert lifestyle is about getting paid well for offering your advice and having so many opportunities flow to you that you never have to "sell" your services again.

How much money you want to make is a different number for just about everyone. It could be six figures or multi-millions a year. The number doesn't really matter as much as the fact that you are making a great living and that you feel financially free. Being financially free is worth more than just making a lot of money. For example, I've been broke and I've also been a millionaire, yet I understand that neither actually guarantees you financial freedom.

Being broke can add a great amount of stress to your life. Often, broke people focus too much on the lack of money they have, and therefore they stay broke.

It takes a massive mind shift to move from broke to a financially free lifestyle. Being a millionaire may feel a lot better, but if you work too hard just to keep up with your lifestyle and/or have no time for your friends and family, it won't feel very free either. That's why financial freedom is the new wealth. It goes beyond money and millions; it's about finding that place in your life where money is no longer your main focus because money flows to you freely. It's a place where you are highly valued and paid well for your services. It is about living an abundant lifestyle with a lucrative and rewarding career that also allows you to personally leave your mark on the world. Clients and opportunity flow to you with ease.

Financial freedom allows you to be free of financial stress and worry, free to choose, and free to make a difference in your own way on your own time.

Set and Visualize Your Expert Goals

It doesn't matter if you are just starting out or if you are reinventing yourself as an expert. Either way you must be able to clearly visualize your future and be able to set focused goals to hit your target.

If you don't know where you are going,
you won't get there.

Here are some questions to help direct you toward your goals:

◆ What do you love doing that you can offer others in the form of a service?

◆ What are you talented or skilled at that can be of service to others?

◆ How do you see your expert career playing out in the future?

◆ What would you like to achieve as a highly paid expert?

◆ How will making more money as an expert change your life?

◆ What is your financial freedom lifestyle goal?

Begin Your Journey Into the World of the Expert

This book is meant to be your guide. In its pages, you will discover a proven step-by-step formula to follow that will allow you to share your wisdom with the world.

You are about to enter the world of the expert, where what you say makes a difference and what you do supports the success of others. As an expert, you have the opportunity to *live* your legacy—not leave it behind. And as a highly paid expert, you live a financially free lifestyle full of opportunity and abundance every day.

Welcome to your new world.

CHAPTER 1

TURN YOUR PASSION, SKILLS, AND TALENT INTO BIG MONEY

You've probably heard the saying, "Do what you love, and the money will follow." Is this actually true? If you follow your passion and pursue what you love doing for a living, will the monetary rewards really follow? What I've discovered is that, although it certainly helps, you'll need more than "doing what you love" to grow a lucrative career in the expert business. Having passion will give you the drive and determination you'll need when the road gets rocky, and skills and talent are required to make a name for yourself as an expert. However, passion, skills, and talent alone won't pay the bills. You also need good business sense and an entrepreneurial mindset to make it to the top of the expert business. Not only are you going to need to stand out, but you'll also need to think outside the box and have a business strategy that moves you to the top.

We all have a life journey, a story, a message, or a skill that will inspire others. What matters most is how we share our message. In business, you must share your powerful message through an innovative brand that quickly sets you apart from the competition. In this critical first step, you will discover how to turn your passion, skills, and talent into becoming a well-known and highly paid expert.

My passion for becoming an expert came from the many wonderful mentors who shaped my life and my career. I launched myself into the expert business to give back. Remember, I had no formal training, only passion when I started out. I didn't even know there was such a thing as a business for experts, and at that time if you called yourself an expert, people felt you were making an exaggerated claim or had a big ego.

Turn Your Passion Into Profits

To turn your passion into a profitable business, you must fulfill a purpose that others need or want. You must find a way to impact others with your knowledge, experience, and/or skills. It isn't enough to have talent; you must master your craft. Allow your passion to fuel your desire to be the best at what you know by blazing your own trail.

Success comes to those who are willing to stay the course despite adversities, challenges, and distractions.

Experts don't give up no matter what mistakes or challenges they need to overcome. In fact, they use their own mistakes as lessons they can teach others to help shorten their learning curve. Experts learn how to achieve their goals, and the goals of others, through perseverance and excellence.

Answer these three important questions to see what drives you:

1. What are you most passionate about that you want to share with others?
2. How will your skills allow you to solve others' problems?
3. How can your talents guide others toward a better personal or professional life?

When your head and your heart are aligned, you make genuine strides in your success.

"Do what you love and the money will follow" is a true statement if you are willing to be patient and persist toward achieving your goals. You must be ready to step up and claim your expertise, and commit to becoming the best that you can be. Never give up on your passion, your dreams, and your pursuit of making a difference. Your message and experiences will make a difference in the lives of others, and making big money will also make a huge difference in your own life. Money gives you the ability to pursue more goals and to give back even more. When you learn to fulfill your dream of living a financially free lifestyle doing what you love every day, you never have to work another day, because doing your work is what you love doing.

Create a Better Business Model

Once I discovered that my passion could make me good money as a speaker, I began to pursue the goal of becoming one of the top marketing speakers in the world. A lofty goal, right? But within a few years, I had achieved this goal and was also honored as one of the top 3 percent of professional women speakers worldwide. Sounds great, but I couldn't help but think, *What's next?* (entrepreneurial thinking here). My business was good, but I realized there must be another way to build an even more lucrative career. I knew there had to be a better business model. At the time, my speaking and consulting business took nearly 100 percent of my personal time. I was so focused on reaching my goals that I didn't stop to think about how dramatically my business income would be affected if something happened to me. This could happen to you too, which is why it's so important to create a business that can run without you if you couldn't be there. Let me ask you this: If you couldn't personally work in your business for a few months, would your income be affected? If you answer yes, you should consider a new way of looking at your overall business model. You don't want to set up a business such that your income is only generated if you are there to run it. You'll need to create what I call your "Personal Life Insurance Policy." It's not actually a written policy, it's simply a business model that allows you to have income flowing into your business without your personal involvement day to day. You need some streams of income that don't require you to be there. This is the way to "insure" that your passion and business remain alive and well for many years to come.

Let me address this in another way. It can be risky if you are always having to chase down new business. This business model can set you up for disaster too. Let me ask you: What if something stopped you from being there to pursue clients? What if you had a health issue or family problems? What would happen then? Now I don't want to be all gloom-and-doom here, but the reality is, life happens! And sometimes life gets in the way of doing business. When this happens, it can be a real game-changer. That's why it's so important to generate additional streams of income that don't require your personal time. There are many ways to pursue your passion without being involved every step of the way. Passions turn to profits when clients and income streams flow easily and consistently *to you*. Your expert streams of income can come from speaking, coaching, consulting, writing, events, developing products, and more—all of these are based around doing what you love to do.

Having a Passion Means Having Choices

As a highly paid expert, you have the opportunity to say yes to things that fill your heart and your pocketbook, and you can also say no to those things that no longer serve you. For example, I walked away and said no to a very lucrative world tour with a business partner because it no longer served my needs and my passion. Once I walked away, I was able to focus on other efforts and other opportunities that were placed at my doorstep. It was a great experience to travel the world and speak in 28 different countries during this time, but the glamour and excitement of international travel began to wear off due to the grueling travel schedule and on-the-go lifestyle. I've always said, "If it's not fun, I'm not going to do it anymore!" This is spoken like a true entrepreneur: entrepreneurs love to create, achieve, and then move on to the next goal or project. Not knowing how to do something has never stopped me or held me back from pursuing my passions. In fact, every business I've ever started, I had little or no experience in. Now, I don't suggest that's a good business model, because it's not. But what I am saying is that if I can do it without a good business plan, you can certainly do it with a proven model and a path to follow.

As an expert, your goal should always be to do business the way it fits your lifestyle. If it doesn't, make a change. This one strategy alone was a real income- and life-changer for my business. For example, I went from making an $8,500 pay day as a paid professional speaker to making *six figures a day* selling my own products from the stage. Nothing changed except for the way I shared my message.

By making more income, I was able to speak and travel less.

Another reason I wanted to get away from the nonstop international travel was to make space to fit someone special into my life. It's pretty hard to meet someone when you have to tell them, "Hey, nice meeting you; I'll see you in a few months when I get back." Most people aren't going to wait around. When I walked away from the world tour, I left space in my life for change and new opportunities to fill that space. I wanted to work closer to my home in Phoenix, Arizona. And once I made that commitment, I set out to change my business model and marketing plan as well. Within a few months, I had met the love of my life, and that sparked a new passion. Now I have a wonderful relationship, and I'm able to make even more money, travel less, and have more time for family and friends.

Being an expert is one of the greatest careers I could have ever imagined. I love making a difference in the lives of others, making a great income, and doing it all my own way. I truly believe that you can manifest anything you want if you focus on it and have a successful plan to follow. Yes, you really can have it all! And not only can you have it all—you can have it all on your own terms!

CHAPTER 2

MASTER YOUR MINDSET

FEAR IS THE BIGGEST OBSTACLE TO PURSUING your dreams. It can stop you in your tracks. Sometimes fear masquerades as excuses that stop your progress. Many people insist it is a lack of money or time or resources, but often it is a fear of failure, rejection, or even of success that holds people back from playing a bigger game in business and in life. Just imagine how much they are missing by allowing an emotion to control their life. You must be willing to step up to turn that passion of yours into a lucrative expert career.

Too many people fail to follow through with their dreams and aspirations in life, mostly because fear holds them back from taking the next step. Why would we allow fear to control us? Mostly because we look at it with short-sightedness: we don't want to be embarrassed, look foolish, be wrong, or make a mistake. What we fear most is fear of the unknown. Yet everything new and exciting is unknown to us at first, and we are destined to fail to some degree; that is only natural.

If you are not scaring yourself, you are playing it too close to your comfort zone.

Fear can also be your friend, and offer you excitement and empowerment. Therefore, if we could think of fear as more of a rush of adrenalin, it could actually catapult us forward and help us accelerate toward lofty goals.

Even successful, confident people are afraid of making changes and trying new things; the difference between successful people and those who are not is that they act in spite of that fear. They feel the fear and move past it. This allows them to feel more confident in return.

Is fear holding you back from achieving your dreams and goals as a highly paid expert? Here are five ways to easily control fear:

1. **Acknowledge your feelings and emotions.** Feelings and emotions can be changed by the words you speak to yourself, so speak kind words of encouragement. Tell yourself that

moving past your fear will reward you with more confidence, knowledge, and personal growth. You are worth it!

2. **Don't waste energy focusing on failure.** Failure is simply a lesson in disguise. With everything new we do, we will experience some level of failure that is necessary to learn and grow both personally and professionally.

3. **Share your fears and ask for support.** When you share your fears with someone, make sure that person is someone who will help you stretch and move outside of your comfort zone. If you share your fears with someone who is also fearful, it can continue to hold you back. Find a support system or a positive mentor whose confidence and success you admire.

4. **Uncover inspiration from books, music, and events.** We all have days when our energy and thoughts are low. Often by taking time to yourself, reading uplifting words, listening to inspiring music, or attending energizing events, you can shift your mood and move to a more positive state of mind.

5. **Feel the fear and act anyway.** The feelings of fear can be worse for us than actually doing the thing we fear. Most of our comfort zones are not all that comfortable anyway—it certainly doesn't feel comfortable when we are stuck. Move outside of it, take a risk, enjoy life to the fullest, and live a life of passion and new

experiences. You must stretch yourself from time to time to keep moving forward.

A Positive Attitude Can Directly Affect Your Success

Your mood reflects onto your personal and business life, and then onto your customers. If you are in a negative mood, it will sweep through your business like wildfire. Experts can't afford to allow negativity to affect their life. Staying positive and enthusiastic is essential to your success. A positive attitude along with contagious enthusiasm will support your groundwork. This groundwork will help to keep the passion burning for your business.

Enthusiasm is contagious—and so is negative energy. In fact, it is even easier for us to pick up negative vibes and reflect them internally in our daily lives. Watch out for negative energy and stay away from negative clients and partners in your business. Being positive will continue to promote your self-esteem and self-belief, and help you avoid negative feelings when times get tough.

Master Your Mindset Exercise

If you find that your mindset needs a little adjusting from time to time, here's an exercise to get you back on track.

Close your eyes, relax, and visualize your complete success, both personally and professionally. Fill your being with the conviction that you are a complete success in this present moment. Imagine that everything you have done this far in life has led you to where you need to be right now. Next, recall and vividly relive some of the most rewarding and successful times in your life. Notice how one thought begins to lead to another as you do this exercise.

Go beyond just memories of success and bring to mind anything that makes you feel good. Get creative. Do this for at least five minutes and note how your energy, emotions, and expectations for yourself have changed their nature. Do you feel more confident, or as if your future looks even more promising?

You are what you think! When you think and feel stronger, you are stronger. The cells and molecules in your body are actually filled with more energy. That's why you feel better.

When you believe in your strengths and abilities, you begin to free up your mind, and you move away from fear and doubt. Everything becomes clearer. Your positive memories, energies, and potentials begin to act immediately to change your capabilities in the present, and you begin to master your mindset again. The expert's mindset takes on many forms. Here are just a few.

◆ **The Disciplined Mind:** Mental discipline is the ability to keep your thoughts focused on goal-directed activity to the exclusion of all else. With high levels of mental discipline, you reach your goals faster.

◆ **The Systemized Mind:** A systemized mind looks at procedures and discovers what needs to be done to make the business work more effectively. With systems in place, you have the ability to see the big picture. Systems allow you to duplicate your success for others.

◆ **The Creative Mind:** The creative mind thinks outside of the box. With creativity, you can discover many unique ways to stand out and move your career ahead.

◆ **The Resilient Mind:** A resilient mind is open and flexible. With an open mind, you let go of uncertainties and become receptive to innovative ideas.

◆ **The Ethical Mind:** An ethical mindset and moral code of conduct is critical to developing lasting relationships. By treating others with respect and fairness, you will develop a respected business reputation.

◆ **The Responsible Mind:** Responsibility holds people accountable. When you are responsible, others will count on you to be dependable, trustworthy, and conscientious.

◆ **The Risk-Taker Mind:** The ability to deal and cope with uncertainty is an important skill set for any expert. Risks come with the acceptance that you will make some mistakes as your business develops. Highly paid experts understand that there is no cookie-cutter model to follow; because experts grow innovative companies, there will always be a certain amount of risk involved. Developing new systems, new products, new presentations, and new events all involve some level of risk. As an expert, you must be open and flexible to taking calculated risks.

CHAPTER 3

EXPERTS INVEST IN OTHER EXPERTS

AS AN EXPERT, YOU HAVE THE RESPONSIBILITY TO continually learn in order to expand your expertise. This is how you support others. Experts are always improving and learning more about their topic of expertise. They continue to grow their expertise by expanding both personally and professionally. They also continually invest in other experts and mentors to minimize their learning curve. If you are not investing in other experts to grow yourself both personally and professionally, how do you expect others to invest in you? This is important, because before you invest heavily in someone else, how can you expect someone to invest heavily in you?

You Can't Grow Your Expert Business Alone

You need ongoing support to keep expanding your expertise, your confidence, and your skills. There is no way I would ever be where I am today without the support of other experts. I have hired experts to assist me in many aspects of my business. What I learn from them is quickly implemented into my own expert business so that it continues to grow. Again, you can't teach what you have not personally experienced, and you can't ask others to invest in you as an expert until you have personally invested in yourself. Until you make a big investment in an expert yourself, you'll probably continue to undervalue your own services and programs, and undervaluing your services will kill your income!

My first big investment in an expert was a scary and exciting experience. I remember how badly I wanted to learn from this expert, yet the $20,000 investment was a bit daunting for me at the time. I had to use a few credit cards to pay it off. Yet, as I look back now on that investment, I understand that I was not investing in any personal time with this expert; I was only investing in his live events—no personal mentoring time. This meant I needed to learn those lessons on my own, and I also had to pay for travel expenses. What I wanted to learn from this expert was how to put on successful events, so I planned on attending the events to see how this expert created such an amazing experience for the audience. As an expert, I wanted to learn a new skill of running a highly successful event business both nationally and internationally.

My investment in that expert soon began to pay off—many times over. The first payoff came when it opened my mind to taking the risk of investing at a much higher level. How can you play a bigger game as an expert if you are not willing to invest in yourself at a higher level? You can't! Making my first large investment shifted my mindset concerning money and my own value, and it allowed me to begin feeling comfortable charging more for my own services. It also taught me a new business model and systems to follow in my own event business.

The next thing I discovered from that investment was that I was gaining more quality clients by attending the events I had invested in. When I attended those events, I found there were more people like myself who had also invested heavily. Therefore, as they got to know me, it was easier for them to invest in my expertise as well. They had already learned the value of investing, so investing with me came easier to them.

If I had to add up the ROI (return on investment) from my initial investment of $20,000, I'm not sure I could come up with an exact dollar value easily. Yet, what I do know is that it's many times higher than what I invested. That investment was paid off quickly by the clients I met at the events who in turn invested in my expertise. It also paid off by giving me the knowledge to expand my own live events in the United States and the confidence to launch my first international event in New Zealand.

If you are wondering, *Why New Zealand?* I answer, *Why not?* I had always wanted to see the beautiful country, and what better way is there to travel the world than by getting paid to speak on your expertise? Most countries in which I've presented welcome international experts with open arms. So I took a chance and signed a contract for a large meeting space in a hotel in downtown Auckland, planning to fill the room. Now this was a very gutsy (or crazy) move because I had no database in that part of the world. Before I left the United States I had arranged for a number of speaking opportunities throughout New Zealand that would help me fill seats for my event (or so I hoped). I had a great time presenting at a few events throughout the country, and I also had an amazing vacation for three weeks! After my speaking tour (a.k.a. my vacation), my assistant and business associate flew in from the United States to meet me in Auckland to help with the live event. Once they arrived, I sent them out to networking groups every day—sometimes they hit two a day— where they signed up more people to attend the event.

My gutsy move paid off. We packed the meeting room and made great sales. This paid for my entire fun vacation and a lot more. I was now in the international event business!

Learn New Skills From Other Experts

As I traveled the world speaking and attending more events, I discovered that there were a lot of new experts coming on the scene. They used speaking as a way to sell their expert services, but they were not professional speakers; in fact, many of them were not even good speakers. But what they did have was a message and an expertise that could help others solve problems, make more money, improve their lifestyle, get more clients, and so on. I saw them selling from the stage like crazy, and they were all making a lot more money than I was at the time. I was already a highly paid and skilled speaker who had been speaking professionally for more than a decade, yet I didn't have the skill of selling well from the stage.

I needed to learn this new model of selling from the stage, and learn it fast. The days of getting booked solid in my paid speaking business began to wane with the economy crisis in the United States. I saved my business income by going international, but for the most part, I was still going from one speech and one country to the next. Always chasing the next speaking engagement was exhausting and not a good entrepreneurial model to grow my company. I knew it was time for me to learn a new skill that would help me gain more income than I had earned as an expert in the past.

At first, I went it alone trying to sell from the stage. I was always good at sales; in fact, I had been selling my entire life. One of my first jobs was selling used rental cars when I was just 20 years old. And if I could sell used rental cars in a tough area of Gary, Indiana, I could sell just about anything—or so I thought.

Sometimes I would sell okay from the stage, but most of the time I was bombing, and walking away with only a handful of sales. It was frustrating trying to learn this skill on my own, and it was costing me dearly in mistakes and my own mental health. I discovered there must be a formula or system that other experts are following to sell from the stage. What was I missing?

That's when I started looking for an expert who could teach me these new selling skills. After being on stage with another speaker/expert who was knocking it out of the park with sales, I asked her how she learned to sell from the stage so well. She said, "I hired an expert for $25,000 to personally teach me his 'speak and sell' formula. And once I got the system down, my sales took off like a rocket." I instantly offered her the same amount of money to teach me what she had learned, but she turned me down. I was shocked! She said, "I would love to take your money, but I would rather turn that investment around by partnering with you in business. You have expert skills that I need to learn: becoming a better speaker, marketing my business more effectively, and putting on my own events." The investment from that brief conversation paid off many times over for both of us. I instantly got her booked on a few stages where I was already scheduled to speak, and we started doing events together that reaped us both a huge return. I learned how to effectively sell from the stage by using a formula that made a huge difference in my sales practically overnight.

Ask yourself these important questions:

1. In what areas of your business do you need to learn from other experts to help you grow and/ or expand into new areas?

2. How can you implement their ideas by adding more value to your own client programs?

Sometimes it's hard to put a value on an investment return. For example, when my mindset shifted concerning investing in other experts to learn new skills, everything changed. It allowed me to move past the fear, doubt, or worry about investing in my own career. That investment ended up being priceless!

Investing in yourself will dramatically shift your mindset forever around the way you value yourself as an expert.

Being an Expert Comes With Responsibility

Becoming an expert comes with a certain amount of responsibility: the responsibility for you to offer a successful program or service, and the responsibility to support others with real, lasting results. To thrive in this business for the long haul, you must be willing to take on this responsibility for yourself and for others.

Being an expert also comes with a certain level of responsibility to be ethical and to give your clients real value. Anyone who chooses to do business with any expert should do some extensive research to check out the expert's reputation and background online before investing. That means people are going to check you out as well. The last thing you want is a tarnished reputation as an expert. It's a small world in the expert business, and if you don't treat people right, the word gets out fast. Growing up, I was taught to always be honest and fair in business. This has always been a top priority for me, and it has served me well. Being honest and ethical in business should be a given, but unfortunately it's not. That's why I must mention it here. You've probably already discovered this for yourself by being burned by some so-called experts.

During the big Internet boom, hundreds of these so-called experts came out of the woodwork like cockroaches. When social media marketing launched, every other person was calling himself a social media expert, yet few of them were real experts creating real value for their clients. Some offered a "magic pill" to getting rich online: They promised that you could make so much money using their system that you could sit on a beach and just watch the money pile up in your bank account. Not only is this unethical, it's illegal; when you make a claim, you had better be able to back it up with solid results!

Set yourself apart as an expert who *always* delivers real value and who follows up with clients and business associates. It drives me absolutely crazy when people don't follow up or do what they say they are going to do. This is also an unprofessional business practice that will kill an expert's opportunities fast. It is your responsibility to not only become a respected expert, but also to align yourself with other highly respected and ethical experts. Experts with a quality reputation are valued for their services, and that will always keep them in high demand.

CHAPTER 4

BUILD A SOLID BRAND FOUNDATION

BUILDING YOUR BRAND IS THE FIRST STEP TO take when you are developing your expert business. Your brand sets the tone of your business and the direction in which it's headed. Or, if you are looking to reinvent or re-design your business, reworking your brand is the first step in redesigning your overall marketing strategy. *What is a brand, and what can it do for me*, you ask? Your brand sets the tone for your overall business image and allows others to quickly understand what your business is all about. Your brand allows others to connect with you, understand what you can do, and recognize that you are the expert in something. Your brand is also the first step toward building trusting relationships with your prospects. Effective branding is critical to moving your business in the right direction. The wrong brand image could put you miles away from your target. You must have a way to stand out instantly to your most ideal target client. In today's noisy marketplace, you *must* stand out from the crowd and be seen as unique and special. Standing out means moving away from the Sea of Sameness to *owning* what you do.

People want to invest in experts they know and trust. Your brand is going to give you that edge. When done effectively, your brand connects to your overall business strategy and your targeted goals. Your brand is everything that represents you and what you are all about. It must work effectively for your overall business image. Once created (or re-created), your brand must remain consistent on every bit of marketing that showcases your business. A complete brand must include an updated logo image, brand colors that match your style, a unique selling message that tells what you do in an instant, and your expert tagline. As you can see, your brand is much more than just a logo. Your brand clearly defines what you do and the benefits you offer to prospects.

Once the overall brand strategy and graphics are created, you'll add them to your business card, e-mail signature, Website, social media, and all marketing materials. Remember, everything must be consistent to keep your brand identity working effectively for you.

Create Your Brand With a Purpose and Mission in Mind

My clients are either new to the expert business or have been working in the business for years. They decide to work with me for different reasons: They want to develop a brand-new business model, or they want to reinvent their existing business model due to the lack of income or sales they desire. Many are looking to completely reinvent themselves and their businesses with a new direction for their expertise and target market. Either way, they always begin with brand foundation.

If they are already doing business as an expert, I begin by evaluating their existing brand, overall business strategy and Website. From there, I can instantly see the blocks in their marketing direction.

When taking on a new or rebranding project, the first place to start is to ask yourself some defining questions. Don't be too general or too grandiose with your answers. Be realistic and honest with yourself as you respond to these questions. As you respond to each question, be specific about your goals and why you want to achieve them. Often, understanding *why* you want to achieve a goal brings more clarity. The more focused you are, the more effective you'll be at developing your overall business and brand strategy. Following are seven important questions to ask yourself before you begin.

1. What sets your business and your expertise apart from your competitors?

2. What unique services do you provide for your clients that other experts don't?

3. What are the top three goals for your business this year?

4. If you could wave a magic wand and change three things in your business right now, what would they be?

5. What are some challenges you are facing today in growing your business?

6. What areas do you need to focus on most to grow your business?

7. What is the long-term vision for your business and expertise?

Establish a Business Name that Showcases Your Expertise

Establish a great business name that defines what your expertise is all about. Here are some example of brand names that I've helped my clients create:

- ◆ Career Transition Expert.
- ◆ Money and Life Freedom Coach.
- ◆ Behavior Change Expert.
- ◆ Breakthrough Life Consulting.
- ◆ The Date Diva.
- ◆ Women's Empowerment Coach.

◆ Awaken to Your Life Purpose.

◆ Stop Dieting for Life.

Once you come up with a good name for your business, make sure the Internet domain name—for example, OneExpert.com—is available. This is very important! You must be able to purchase the dot-com. And if the dot-com domain name is not available, change the business name! This is a critical first step because once you get into brand domination online, you won't be able to dominate your market without owning the dot-com domain name along with other similar Website names. It's extremely important that you grab those Website names at the time your business name is developed. Don't do anything else until you own the dot-com for your business and your brand. This is a critical first step that a lot of marketing experts won't even tell you about.

Many of my clients are located outside of the United States, and therefore they pick a domain that is known within their country, such as *www.expert.ca* for Canada, *www.expert.au* for Australia, *www.expert.br* for Brazil, and so on. That's fine; grab the country domain for your business, but you also need to buy *www.expert.com*. Because it's a dot-com world! The ".com" is the most recognized symbol throughout the world. You want to make it easy for anyone to remember your domain, and ".com" is internationally known.

Furthermore, as an expert, you want to launch yourself to the world—not just your own country. For example, my client Helena who lives in Australia was in the process of launching her weight-loss business called Simple Slimming when she hired me to work with her to grow her business. Luckily, she had not yet launched her Website, because we had to go back and start from the beginning with a new business name since she didn't own the dot-com. Helena had only purchased the domain for her country of Australia (.au). She had selected a good name for her business, and for that reason she didn't want to give it up, but from our very first call together, I discovered that she wanted to eventually grow her business outside of Australia, and I knew she would have a problem with the business name down the road if she didn't own the dot-com. Once I convinced Helena to *own* a business name for which she could have the dot-com and therefore have more Internet domination, she agreed to change her business name.

During our first mentoring call, we searched online for keywords and domains as we "brand-stormed" new ideas for her business name. We knew we had to come up with a great name, and that's when we discovered Winning at Slimming was available. I told Helena it was great, and told her, "Grab it! Buy it right now before it's gone!" Once she purchased the domain WinningAtSlimming.com, we also discovered more dot-coms along with her country code domains that she could hold on to as her business grew. These included StartSlimmingNow.com and StartSlimmingToday.com, which we used for her landing page Websites.

This is how brand and business strategy go hand in hand: You must know where you are going. Plan to take your brand and your business global once you launch or re-launch your brand name, or you'll have a hard time owning your space online.

Develop or Redevelop an Effective Logo

The logo is one of the most critical parts of an effective business brand. Therefore, before you set out to create a new logo or re-create an existing logo, you need to first understand what a logo is and how it builds your brand awareness.

A logo identifies a company or product with the use of an image, text style, or design. Logos are designed to identify your business at first glance. A logo should not just describe what a business does; it should also identify the business in a memorable and simplistic way. Only after a logo becomes familiar does it function effectively. Before beginning your logo design, ask yourself these questions:

♦ What do you want your logo to symbolize about your business?

♦ What visual do you want to create that prospects can quickly and easily relate to?

Following are seven tips for creating an effective logo

1. **Keep it simple and memorable.** A simple logo design allows for easy recognition and allows the logo to be versatile and memorable. Effective logos feature something unexpected or unique without being overdone. An effective

logo design should also endure the test of time as your company grows.

2. **Engender emotions and feelings about your quality and company principles.** Think about what emotion or feelings you would like your logo to create in a prospect's mind. Perhaps feelings of joy and happiness, trust and loyalty, comfort in quality service, safety, warmth, fun, winning, or motivation. Consider what qualities you would like your logo to bring to mind as well. Perhaps beautiful, elegant, bright, simple, striking, or conservative. Also keep in mind what principles or truths you would like to showcase in your design. Perhaps overall vision or direction, consistency, reputation, quality, or years in business.

3. **Select the right colors.** Color is like a silent language that can motivate, persuade, or turn prospects off in an instant. People actually respond more to nonverbal cues than verbal ones. That is why color triggers a variety of emotions and memories. Be sure to utilize the best colors that showcase your business and speak to your target market effectively.

4. **Choose the right font.** Choosing the right font can make or break a good design. Spend some time researching all the various fonts that could be used for your project. Think about what image you want the font to create. Do you want flowing script, or corporate and traditional?

Slim or bold text? Strong or soft? Maybe you need one that appeals specifically to a male or female market.

5. **Get good ideas from other successful logos.** Check out other logos to help you brainstorm ideas and get a direction for your own unique design. Google Images is a great place to search for ideas. But make sure you use other logos for *ideas only.* Do not steal, copy, or borrow other design ideas. Do not use stock or clip art either. The point of your logo is to be unique and original.

6. **Use multiple graphic artists to develop a variety of designs.** Onc of my favorite resources for logo design is 48HoursLogo.com. This Website is set up as a contest for multiple graphic designers to compete for your logo design. You don't have to spend much to get a lot of choices, and the artists are great at following your design suggestions and adjustments until your logo is finalized. The logo design process can be fun and fast, but making the final decision may be somewhat of a challenge without the right outside support.

7. **Ask for support on your final logo design.** Often we are so close to our own businesses that we don't see the obvious. A prospect has a different viewpoint about your business than you do; that's why getting some outside help to define your logo image is important. Now,

that doesn't mean going out and asking all your friends and family to give their opinions. They most certainly will have an opinion, but will it be the right one? If you get the wrong advice, it may hurt you and hold up the process of getting your design completed. I suggest that you work only with a marketing or branding expert to help you define and finalize your logo image. Your logo design will set the tone of your business image; therefore it's critical you get it right before creating or re-creating your overall marketing brand.

The "Build Your Brand Foundation" Toolbox

A clearly defined brand is the foundation of your business. It is what articulates the authenticity and characteristics of your business. It is what differentiates your business in the marketplace. The purpose of a brand platform is to ensure consistency in how your brand is communicated. Your brand is what allows you to build recognition, trust, and loyalty.

Remember that a nicely designed logo or slick brochure is just *one* aspect of your brand. Your brand has a voice. Your brand is your "everything," it is affected by the way you communicate both internally and externally. All the elements of your brand must be consistent on your Website, social media, business cards, and everywhere else. This consistency is critical to leverage your brand to its fullest potential.

Every aspect of your brand reflects on you as "the expert." So, whether you are building your brand from the ground up or remodeling, your brand is the foundation for your success. Here are the most important tools for building our all-important brand.

Your Brand Toolbox

Utilize the Psychology of Color

The use of color and images in your brand logo has a lasting impact on whether a prospect will decide to work with you. Color in marketing speaks loudly in the sub-conscious mind, and it can cause a positive or negative reaction in your prospect in a matter of seconds. On the Internet, where you don't deal face to face with potential clients, you have less than 30 seconds to connect and make a great first impression. Therefore, the words (or sales copy) on your Website have, by far, the greatest psychological impact on your visitors, and thus they become your most important communication and marketing tool. But another important psychological aspect of your Website that's often overlooked is the colors. Just as you use words to express yourself, colors can be used as an expression as well. Color is a language of its own. The background color of your Website, the color of your banner, and the color of your text, bolded headlines, and sub-headlines all have a psychological impact on your visitors.

Color is like a silent language that can motivate and persuade or demotivate and turn off prospects in an instant. People actually respond more to nonverbal cues than verbal ones. Therefore, make sure to utilize the psychology of colors (detailed in the following list) in all your marketing and branding consistently, in everything you do, from your Website to your business card, social media, advertising, and so on.

When color is used correctly, it can send a number of messages to your prospects. It can also highlight important points. However, if used incorrectly, color can quickly confuse your prospects and lead them away from your marketing message altogether. Colors trigger a variety of emotions and memories. To know which colors will appeal to your prospects, you must understand your target market well. Following is a list of some of the common colors and what type of emotion they invoke in people.

◆ **Black** is associated with seriousness, authority, power, and boldness; it is distinguishing and classic. Business-wise, it's great for creating drama. When overused on Websites, it is too hard on the eyes, so it should be utilized as an accent or text color only (not for backgrounds).

◆ **Blue** is associated with trustworthiness, success, security, authority, seriousness, and professionalism. When utilized in business, dark blue or navy is best because it showcases responsibility and power. A lighter blue may showcase calmness.

◆ **Brown** is associated with earth, nature, simplicity, richness, politeness, helpfulness, and effectiveness. Light brown implies genuineness whereas dark brown is similar to wood or nature. It is a good neutral color but should be used sparingly in marketing so that it doesn't provoke a dark or negative impression.

◆ **Gray** is associated with authority, professionalism, a reserved nature, practicality, earnestness, and creativity. Business-wise it is very traditional and conservative but can make a great accent color for a more corporate organization.

◆ **Green** is associated with health, freedom, freshness, healing, the environment, tranquility, nature, and harmony. It is a calming, refreshing color when utilized effectively and not overused.

◆ **Orange** is associated with celebration, fun, youth, affordability, and excitement. When utilized in business, it is good for highlighting information, yet it can also showcase a discount, so use it sparingly and effectively. There are different shades of orange that will create different emotions. Dark burnt orange, for example, can fit well with greens and browns and create a more natural, calming feeling.

◆ **Pink** is associated with softness, sweetness, innocence, youthfulness, femininity, gentleness, and well-being. For business, you must be aware of its feminine links and implications.

◆ **Purple** is associated with spirituality, royalty, luxury, wealth, sophistication, authority, and even fantasy. In business, it is upscale and works with artistic types. It can also appear to be a more feminine and emotional color.

◆ **Red** is associated with excitement, strength, love, passion, impulse, action, adventure, vitality, and aggressiveness. It commands attention. When utilized in business, it showcases boldness and emotion. It works well as a strong accent color. Dark red or burgundy can soften the emotions and may create a more professional image if used for more than just an accent color.

◆ **White** is associated with purity, cleanliness, devotion, contemporary themes, and simplicity. For business, it can be anything from sterile to refreshing. It's good for basic highlighting and balance in your marketing copy.

◆ **Yellow** is associated with playfulness, warmth, sunshine, cheer, happiness, curiosity, and amusement. It appeals to the intellectual types and is a good accent. Yellow enhances concentration (hence its use in legal pads). Goldenrod yellow is one of the best sales conversion rate colors to utilize online and also for direct mail. It is also the most difficult color for the eye to take in, so it can be overpowering if overused.

Remember, it's not only your words that psychologically impact the subconscious minds of your prospects, it's also your use of color. (We'll discuss how to choose each word of your marketing and branding wisely and how to speak directly to your target market in benefit-rich language in more detail later in the book.)

CHAPTER 5

STAND OUT TO GROW

Developing your unique selling proposition, or USP, requires some focused brainstorming and creativity; this is what I call "Brand-Storming." This process requires careful analysis of your unique message and your most ideal clients. When you analyze in detail what you have to offer, beyond your products or services, you can learn a great deal about how to distinguish yourself from the competition.

You must develop a statement that clearly defines what your *brand promise* is, and what makes you stand out. That may sound easy, but your brand promise can be a challenging message to define because you are so close to your own business that you can't easily see the most obvious things that someone on the outside may see. It takes an outside prospective to come up with a message that clearly defines what your business has to offer and what makes you unique.

Put Yourself in Your Prospect's Shoes

Too often, experts fall in love with their product or service offerings and forget that it is the customers' needs, not their own, that they must satisfy. You need to step back and carefully scrutinize what your customers really want. Pricing is never the only reason people don't buy. If you are having a hard time standing out because competitors are beating you out on price, you probably have a problem with your value message. You must communicate your marketing message in the form of value-driven benefits. Respond to the following questions, and be brutally honest with your answers.

◆ What benefits do you bring to your customers that your competitors do not?

◆ Why is your program, system, or service more innovative, unique, or special?

Effective marketing requires you to be an amateur psychologist: You need to know what drives and motivates prospects to turn them into buyers. You must touch their emotional buttons. Reasons for a person's emotional buying could be that he is feeling some type of pain in his business and/or professional life; another big reason may be that he isn't getting the results he desires and other experts have not fulfilled his needs. So stop selling and start listening. How are you going to motivate your prospects to buy if you don't know what they really need? Your marketing message won't sell unless it makes a connection. Start asking your prospects and existing customers what their needs are. You'll be surprised by how honest they are when you ask them how you can improve your service or offerings.

If your business is just starting out, you won't have a lot of customers to ask for feedback, so the best way to know what prospects are looking for is to shop your competition online. Do some extensive research and find out who your competition is, and then create a new marketing prospective by shopping them. Clear your mind of any preconceived ideas about your own product or service (such as, "It's the best ever!"), and be brutally honest with yourself about what you are about to see at your competitors' Websites. Pay close attention to what they are using to make themselves stand out. Then go one better!

Don't get discouraged with the process of developing your USP. It takes concentration and a clear focus to create your unique marketing message. Start out by making a list of all the benefits and solutions you provide for your customers. Then write out numerous messages using these benefit- and solution-oriented words until you can finalize your message down to a three- to 15-word statement that emphasizes your benefits and results. Make it simple for your prospects to understand and quickly relate to.

Moving Up the Ranks With Your Expertise

As your brand and marketing messages become clearer, you'll begin to gain more clients. This will allow your career and your income to move up. It doesn't matter where you start, as long as you have the goal of reaching the top to become a highly paid expert. I call this reaching the top of the pyramid. Take a look at the pyramid image on the next page. It illustrates the different levels an expert goes through as she develops and grows her business. Notice that the bottom of the pyramid is the widest—that's where the majority of the competition is. It's harder to compete and make money there. As you move up the pyramid it gets smaller. And as the pyramid gets smaller your opportunities and income increase due to more recognition and less competition.

As you move up to higher levels as an expert, you become more well-known to your niche market, and more opportunities come your way. The results are always the same as you move up: you develop higher-priced programs and services, and create additional streams of income. Your goal should be to get to the top as quickly and as professionally as you can!

At the very bottom of the pyramid is the **novice**. This is someone who is new to the expert business. This is a beginner level where the expert starts out as a commodity

until he develops a uniqueness and direction for his expertise that makes him stand out. At this level, the beginner has a lot of competition because his level of expertise and/or brand has not yet been fully developed. Therefore he needs to keep his prices lower in order to compete. At this level, the beginner is still developing his brand and learning the ropes. Oftentimes, beginners complain that they have a problem getting clients who can afford their services. This is because at this level, the novice has not built up enough value for his prospects to recognize just yet.

The second level is **skilled**. The skilled expert has learned a bit more and has developed skills that set her apart, yet she probably isn't getting the high-end clients she wishes for just yet. When a skilled expert is at this level, she may have some branding and marketing in place, and may have even landed some clients, but her income doesn't match her skill level. The reason for this is often poor marketing that is not getting the word out and promoting her effectively. In this case, she needs to go back and reinvent her marketing efforts to direct more targeted clients so she can move to the next level.

The third level is **specialist**. When an expert reaches this level he has developed a name for himself within a specific industry or field. At this level, the expert begins to move ahead of the competition. As he becomes known as a specialist, the competition begins to fall away. The specialist may be more in demand as he move up the pyramid, and as his demand increases, he begins to charge more for his services and does more specialized work. Having a specialty allows the expert to go narrower and deeper and really hone in on mastering his craft. This allows him to deliver at a higher level, and therefore his value and income increases.

The fourth level is **authority**. Experts at this high level generate steady streams of income at higher prices than the average specialist. They begin to generate more income because they get more money by positioning themselves as an authority in their niche market. For an expert to position herself as an authority, she must have already developed proven systems and results for her clients. She most likely has case studies and powerful video testimonials from her clients to prove the results she produces. At this level the expert begins to limit her availability to work one-on-one as she increases her fees for private coaching/consulting sessions and VIP client days.

The top level is what every expert strives for: **highly paid expert**. When the expert achieves this level, he now has top-level brand equity and a higher perceived value. He has a large following of raving fans, allowing him to easily launch new products, programs, events, joint venture partners, and much more. He has developed high-end services and has hooked high-level clients. He lives a financially free lifestyle, and new clients and income-generating opportunities continue to flow to him with ease. Life is good at the top!

CHAPTER 6

CREATE YOUR EXPERT CALLING CARD

AFTER YOUR LOGO AND USP HAVE BEEN ESTABLISHED or reinvented, it's time to move on to your first marketing piece: your business card. Most cards don't accurately present what someone's business is all about. I am shocked by how many bad business cards I see out there. And I know if there is a problem with the business card, the rest of the marketing is likely to be a disaster too.

Your business card may be the first visual connection a prospect has to your business. Your card will either promote or demote your professional image. As an expert, you can't afford to get this wrong. People will be judging you at first glance, and your card will quickly showcase the level of success you have in your business. If a prospective customer views your business image as unprofessional or confusing in any way, he simply won't show interest in what you have to offer.

I've seen very few business cards that send a clear message that would make me jump at the chance of doing business with this person. Most cards are simply used for contact information and miss the mark on marketing all together. Most lack a strong visual logo, branded image, or benefit-rich statement plus a strong call to action.

Having effective marketing is critical to building your expert brand.

The goal of your business card is to make a powerful first impression. It must do three things:

1. Visually showcase what you do.

2. Share a message that sets you apart from the competition.

3. Offer a call to action to get the prospect to your Website.

Most of us are so close to our business that we don't see the most obvious mistakes that could be costing us in lost clients. We don't always look at our business through our prospects' eyes, but only through a very narrow focus— our own. Because of this myopia, a great place to start improving your business image is to take a close look at the business card you already have as if you were a prospective customer who knew nothing about your business. Compare your card with my Top 10 Business Card Mistakes in the following list, and then take my quick Business Card Improvement Quiz.

The Top 10 Most Common Business Card Mistakes

1. The images on it are scrambled, with inconsistent design elements.

2. Your services and/or products are not clearly defined.

3. It does not showcase what's unique about you or your business.

4. Your expert brand and/or tagline doesn't stand out or is not professional.

5. It indicates unflattering things about your business.

6. It has no call to action to connect a prospect to your Website.

7. It gives a cluttered impression with mixed messages.

8. It's filled with non-essential information or omits important marketing content.

9. It looks out of date or unprofessional.

10. It lacks a point of interest and doesn't easily connect to the prospect.

How does your card rank?

Answer these 16 questions to see how your card ranks. Simply answer yes to all that apply. Be honest with yourself. Then count all your *yes* responses and score your business card.

1. Does your card present a positive, interesting, and professional image overall?

2. Does your card feature an updated, professionally designed logo?

3. Does your logo make a good visual connection with your business image?

4. Does your card have a USP or marketing message that best describes your business?

5. Is the font and text size easy to read at a glance?

6. Does your card offer a call to action to get prospects to your Website?

7. Does your card extend a free expert offer to get prospects to your Website?

8. Are all of your marketing materials consistent with your business card image?

9. Is your Website featured in bold text to stand out?

10. Has your business card been updated in the past year?

11. Are you utilizing the back of the card for additional marketing information?

12. Does your card feature your expert tagline that describes your unique expertise?

13. Do you feature your photo on your card to make a personal connection?

14. Do you often receive compliments on your business card?

15. Do prospects show interest right away and ask you more about your services?

16. Do you act upon every opportunity to proudly pass out your card?

Now count all of your *yes* answers and see how your card ranks:

16–13 Yes Responses: You have a professional business card that will help you turn more prospects into buyers.

12–9 Yes Responses: Your business card needs some work. Redesign your card to help you stand out as a professional expert.

8 or Fewer Yes Responses: The business image you are projecting is costing you opportunities. Get to work! Reevaluate and redesign your business card and all of your marketing materials to improve your prospective opportunities and income.

Set Up Your Expert Calling Card Design

Now that you've rated your business card, you may realize it's time to create a new design. But first, you must have completed all of your branded images and USP statement before starting your new business card design. And if you don't have an updated photo of yourself, schedule a professional photo shoot to have a new headshot image created for the front of your card. If *you* are the personal brand of your business, this will give your card a personal connection to you as the expert.

On the front of your card, you'll want to list your USP message at the very top. This will tell prospects instantly what you are all about, rather than making them try to figure it out on their own. Under the USP message, post your new logo and your photo. Under the photo, add your name and professional credentials. Under that you may also want to add your tagline, such as *Professional Speaker, Author, Consultant*, or *Expert*. You could also use a branded tagline as I do: *The Expert of Experts*. Create a branded tagline of your own that makes you instantly recognizable to your target market.

At the bottom front of your card, list your e-mail address and phone number. Your physical address is optional, unless clients must come to your location. Next, create a call to action such as this: "Contact us to learn more about our programs and services at YourBusiness. com."

Utilize the space on the back of the card for another call to action, such as highlighting a free offer on your Website to get prospects to sign up. You free offer may be a guidebook, an e-book, a special report, or an audio program. Create a call to action such as this: "Get your FREE Guidebook," and list your Website below it. Add the Web address of your corporate Website or landing page and create a data capture from leads that come from your business card. It's always good to have a visual, so add an image of your free offer. Another item to add would be a QR code that directs prospects directly to your Website from their smart phone. Prospects will then be able to easily scan the code to go to your Website instantly. To create a free QR code for your card (and to check out other offline marketing materials) go to *www.qrstuff.com*.

Your improved expert card will instantly start connecting with more prospects and get them to take the right action that builds your database. Your card will showcase your brand effectively and feature *you* as the go-to expert. It will also offer a strong call to action for prospects to go to your Website to instantly learn more about you and your expertise. Your networking opportunities will instantly improve as well.

CHAPTER 7

YOU ARE THE BRAND

THE SKILLS EXPERTS LEARN ARE OFTEN DEVELOPED from their own real-life experiences. If your skills and experiences don't match your authentic brand direction, you're going to hit a wall when you go after ideal clients and expect big money from your marketing efforts.

For example, I've had a few students say to me, "I want to be a wealth-building or money expert." But the problem they all had was that *they had not personally built their own wealth*. It's hard to claim you are a wealth-building expert if you haven't already created massive wealth for yourself.

In fact, some so-called wealth-building experts I've met are actually *broke*! Those people may have learned a lot about making money by reading books or interviewing a lot of wealthy people, but they're not experts at it if they haven't done it for themselves.

How could you possibly support others as a credible expert on something you have not personally experienced? You can't! But when you do have the background and credibility to launch an expert brand, your business can get launched rather quickly. Because *you* are your brand!

Take my client Penny Dyer, for example. She has been in the college and university market for many years and she knows and relates to that specific niche industry. She has the skill and experience to become a well-known expert in that market. So it only made sense that she would select this area to grow her personal brand under the name of UniversityByDesign.com. Penny also discovered that there was a void in this market. That's when she decided to become the go-to expert to help her clients get into the colleges of their choice. She now helps students overcome the challenges of getting into the right university. Penny took a brilliant business idea, and then added her passion for supporting others and her academic background to build a successful coaching business. As an expert, she now helps shape the futures of students (and their parents) from around the world. Penny has the skill and experience to create real results. After working with students from around the world, many have been able to get unsolicited scholarships in colleges in the United States for as much as $80,000 to $90,000—all due to the quality of their work submitted during the application process taught by Penny's company, University by Design.

Get Really Good at Promoting *You*

Once you figure out how *you* will best represent your overall brand, the next step is to get really good at marketing yourself. I call this "shameless self-promotion."

Self-promotion, when done effectively, works for any business or career. Once you begin to implement the proven marketing strategies behind it, it's much easier to be successful in anything you set your mind to. In fact, when you get good at promoting yourself and your services, you will also begin to enjoy it more. Self-promotion can become very rewarding.

When I was writing my book *Confessions of Shameless Self-Promoters*, I was shocked to discover that an average of 85 percent of the thousands of business owners, entrepreneurs, and experts I've surveyed around the world did not feel comfortable promoting themselves and avoided it most of the time. Yet, in business we understand that if we don't promote and market, we can't be successful. No matter how great your product or service is or what amazing value you offer, if prospects don't know about you, you're not going to win the opportunity to do business with them. Therefore, not promoting yourself goes against the grain of all sales and marketing success!

Why do so many people feel uncomfortable with self-promotion? Because much of what they believe to be true about self-promotion comes from past programing that dates back to childhood. Too many of us have negative and/or limited beliefs rattling around in our heads about the concept of self-promotion. These limiting and negative beliefs have been programed into our subconscious minds for 10, 20, 30, or more years.

Ask yourself these questions:

◆ What were your parents, teachers, or guardians like when you were growing up? Did they believe in promoting themselves?

◆ Did they promote your self-esteem to believe that you could do anything you set your mind to?

◆ Were they risk-takers, or were they conservative?

◆ Did you ever hear comments such as, "It's not polite to talk about yourself"?

Knowing the answers to these questions may help you remove some blocks that may be holding you back from putting yourself out there and shamelessly promoting yourself.

We may hate to admit it, but many of us are creatures of habit, especially when habits have been programed into our brains since childhood. Some of us are so conditioned against self-promotion that our minds may be closed to it, no matter how much it could benefit us. Now, I don't expect you to change your beliefs about this overnight, but you can start by opening your mind to believing differently about self-promotion from this day forward with some tips I'm about to share with you.

Why believe differently about promoting yourself? Because you can't be truly successful as an expert if you aren't willing to let people know that you, your product, and/or your services exist. Period! If you aren't willing to promote your talents, expertise, and products, others will quickly pass you by. The world is not going to beat a path to your door; you have to pave the way.

Resenting self-promotion is one of the greatest obstacles to success!

Writing my book on the topic of shameless self-promotion helped me to build a bigger and stronger brand for myself, and it changed everything for my expert business. That book launched my career as a best-selling author and international expert on self-promotion. Because I was already branded as a marketing expert, it was the thing that made me stand out from other marketing experts. Here's exactly how I did it.

Just after the first edition of *Confessions of Shameless Self-Promoters* was published, I took out an ad in *Radio TV Interview Report*. The half-page advertisement ran for three months and kept my phone ringing for more than *six* months with requests for interviews from radio shows all over the United States and Canada. The headline of my ad read, "This Guest Can Make Anyone Shamelessly Famous!" Radio producers started calling me right away asking me to be a guest expert on their shows. One of those calls turned out to be a request for a live interview with shock jock Howard Stern.

When I picked up the phone the producer said, "This is K.C. Armstrong from *The Howard Stern Show*. We heard about your book *Confessions of Shameless-Self Promoters*, and we want to have Howard interview you on his show. Are you interested?" At first I thought it was one of my friends playing a prank on me, but felt I should play along just in case it was the real deal. "Howard is going to beat me up," I said. "Oh, no!" said K.C. Part of me really wanted to believe him, but I knew better; his is definitely not your typical radio interview show. Howard's show is all about controversy, with two or three interviewers ganging up on the guest, looking for something outrageous to talk about. You've really got to be on your toes to survive an interview like this. Without taking any time to think about it, I heard these words come flying out of my mouth: "Sure, I would *love* to be on Howard's show!"

When I hung up I thought to myself, *What the heck did I get myself into now?* As I pondered the idea, I reminded myself that as a motivational speaker I'd been teaching people for years how to step outside of their comfort zones and create gutsy goals that make them stretch. And this sure was a stretch for me!

The interview was going to be in a month, so I had time to seek out some supportive advice from another expert. The first person I called was Bill Goss. Bill wrote a book called *The Luckiest Unlucky Man Alive* after surviving 30 near-death experiences. I had included his story in my book, and I remembered him telling me that he was on *The Howard Stern Show* himself for more than an hour talking about one of his accidents. Howard had some fun with Bill's story, talking about his nurses, and...well, you don't want to know what else. Anyway, I knew that Bill could give me some solid advice on how to survive an interview like this. When I talked with Bill, I asked if I could call him every week until my scheduled show time. He agreed, and each week he coached me through different scenarios, discussing every possibility of how the interview might go.

"You will probably only get a couple of minutes on the show," Bill told me, "and then he is going to hang up on you. The *best* you'll get is five decent minutes if you handle it well. And believe me, you don't want any more time with him than that." Okay, so now my biggest challenge was to get no more than five challenging minutes of fame with the shock jock. *I can do that!* I thought. I was ready for just about any direction this interview could go, and was also ready to feed Howard's ego a bit, because I knew that would get him on my side. I can't say that I respect everything about Howard Stern, but I *do* respect the fact that he is a famously successful self-promoter who lives by the three rules of shameless success:

1. **Have your own style.** No one can compete with you when you are comfortable enough being your own person, sharing your own ideas and your own mind.

2. **Never give up,** no matter how many roadblocks get in your way. Move around them, over them, or through them, and just keep going.

3. **Find a way to position yourself** in front of people who can support your success.

You've got to admit that Howard is a shameless survivor! And after my 4.5-minute interview, I was a survivor too. (And yes, just in case you were wondering, I did keep my clothes on and my professionalism intact!) Howard promoted the book by saying, "Hey, everybody needs to be more shameless about what they do to become successful. And if you want to find out how, buy this book." My shortest and most challenging interview took my book *Confessions of Shameless Self-Promoters* to best-seller on Amazon.com within a matter of hours. Wow!

I now believe there is no such thing as bad publicity when you know how to position yourself effectively to the media. Often the more outrageous or fun your interview is, the more publicity you will get in return. So don't be afraid; just be yourself and have some fun with it. For example, I created a press release about my interview on Howard's show to get even more publicity for my book and expertise. Here it is:

For Immediate Release! Media Shock Jock vs. The Shameless Marketing Diva

Who: The World's Most Challenging Radio Interviewer

Shock jock Howard Stern is known for his outrageous and controversial topics. His guests must be ready for anything if they want the interview to promote them in a positive way. Staying on top of the interview game is not easy. Nervous guests go one against three difficult radio hosts at the same time. Many of his guests have been known to fail miserably and are put down or even attacked during the show. Few guests have turned around the interview in their favor and made it a success. Debbie Allen, the author of *Confessions of Shameless Self-Promoters*, did just that when she was featured on a live radio interview with Howard Stern, who has 10 million followers from coast to coast.

The Shameless Marketing Diva Wins Over the Interview

Self-promotional marketing expert Debbie Allen not only survived the interview, but she did it famously. The interview started in a negative tone, but soon Debbie turned it around in her favor. Howard Stern, a shameless self-promoter himself, challenged the "Shameless Diva" on the title that grabbed his attention: "This Guest Can Make Anyone Shamelessly Famous." "So who are you?" he asked her. "If you can make anyone famous how come I haven't heard of you?"

said Howard. Debbie came back with, "I'm on your show and you know who I am now, right?" Debbie managed to turn the interview around in her favor, and the next thing she knew Howard was asking her to share some of her best tips from the book for his listeners to learn from. He did admit, "Now I'm not like Oprah's book of the month club. I don't promote books; especially business books. But I believe you've got something good going so I'm going to promote you." He then gave out the title of the book and told people to go on Amazon.com to buy it.

What: Debbie, a.k.a. The Shameless Marketing Diva, discovered that by connecting with Howard's interests, understanding the show, and by being coached, she would survive the world's most challenging radio show host. Not only did she survive, she thrived from the massive media exposure. Within a few hours of being on the show her book *Confessions of Shameless Self-Promoters* hit Amazon's bestseller list.

Where: Line up Debbie Allen, The Shameless Marketing Diva, for your show today. She can handle any interview challenge, and she might even help you get shamelessly famous too. Contact us at 855-2-DEBBIE or via her online press room at DebbieAllen.com.

If you don't toot your own horn,
you can't enjoy the music!

In business we understand that if we don't promote and market, we can't be successful. Right? No matter how great your service is or what amazing value you offer, if prospects don't know about you, you're not going to win the opportunity to do business with them. Therefore, if you don't promote yourself…it goes against the grain of all sales and marketing success!

Some people are so conditioned against self-promotion that they are closed minded about it; no matter how much it might benefit them. Now, I don't expect you to change your belief over night, but you can start by opening your mind to believing differently about self-promotion from this day forward. Why believe differently? Because you can't be truly successful as an expert if you aren't willing to let people know that you, your product, and/or services exist? If you aren't willing to promote your talents, expertise, and products, opportunities will quickly pass you by. The world is not going to beat a path to your door unless you pave the way.

CHAPTER 8

STAY ON TARGET

DISJOINTED MESSAGES SENT TO THE WRONG prospects will quickly kill your marketing efforts. Trying to be everything to everyone does not allow you to make a difference or stand out; it's nearly impossible to define your ideal target market that way.

You must relate to your ideal clients and target market with everything you do! Once you complete your logo, select your colors, and finalize your USP and everything else that defines your brand, your marketing will be targeted toward a very specific group of prospects. Every time the right prospect lands on your Website or social media links, she will understand exactly what your expertise is all about.

Here are six steps to keep you on target in your business

◆ **Step 1: Always be marketing.** If you launch your expert business before perfecting the marketing of your brand, it's going to be challenging to get new clients who value your work. Sometimes a few slight adjustments in your marketing can open up a lot more doors of opportunity for you. For example, my client Denise Turner was already a successful color therapist expert when she started working with me. She had high-level corporate clients and her business was already running well, for the most part. All I did was tweak some of her existing marketing so that she could be more on target. Together we looked at every word and image on her Website, and then adjusted the pieces that needed to change. Now that she's more on target, her marketing gains her more ideal clients with ease.

◆ **Step 2: Get serious about your business.** An expert is serious about playing a bigger game in business and in life. Everything you do needs to be perfectly aligned to target only ideal clients who pay you well for your services. Here are some examples of this:

Example #1: Whether you're speaking for free or for a fee, you must have the goal of making money from your presentation. It will be your main goal.

Example #2: Every marketing piece should have a strong call to action that leads people to do business with you in some way. Experts run their business like a real business, not a hobby.

◆ **Step 3: Develop systems that save you time.** As an expert, you must learn to get focused on your business at all times. Clients often say to me, "How are you able to respond to all of your clients so quickly? How do you get it all done?" I'm extremely focused and have developed systems for customer service and follow-ups. Clients love it when you follow up, especially after the sale.

Develop a working system that allows you to save time for the important parts of running your business. For example, one of the ways I save time is by never answering the telephone, unless I have a scheduled appointment. The telephone is such a time-waster unless it's a planned and focused call. Every call has a time-line and agenda to follow. I respond to my clients the majority of time via e-mail unless we have a personalized mentoring call scheduled. My personal clients are even trained on how to respond to me via e-mail by asking one question or one focused topic per e-mail. This helps save both of us time and allows for fast response time. Also, my telephone service is set up on a system that sends me an instant e-mail with the recorded voice message in an attached file.

I can click on the message from my computer or my cell phone and decide if the call needs to be returned by me or my assistant. If my assistant can handle the call, I simply forward the e-mail to her to follow up. This way every call or e-mail that comes into my office is followed up within 24 hours or less.

You must develop systems similar to these that save you time and run your business productively. Your clients should never have to hear the excuse that you were too busy. Many experts work from a home office and have a virtual assistant or staff who handles much of the follow-up work. I have two assistants: one for personal client call follow-up, and another for my online support and back office.

◆ **Step 4: Get productive.** Doing unproductive things is a huge time-waster. I always say that if you want to achieve your goals, focus on doing three things every day that will help you get to your main goal. When you focus on doing things that grow your business instead of working on details you could delegate to someone else, you can achieve your goals much faster.

◆ **Step 5: Stay focused on your goals.** There's that word again: *focus*! You must have clear goals about what you want to teach others, and just stay focused on that all the time. Selecting the right clients to work with will also keep you focused. For example, if you decide to work with the wrong type of client just because you can make money from them, it may cost you twice as much in time in the long run. Every time you take on an unfocused client or a client who's a pain to deal with, you undervalue your services and waste your time. Highly paid experts know to say yes only to the most ideal clients and opportunities, especially if they offer personalized coaching or consulting services. When you reach this level as an expert, you feel more confident in your direction and it's easier to say no to the wrong prospect.

◆ **Step 6: Ask for help so you can stay on target.** If you need help getting the right prospects, you need to *ask* for help. You can't be an expert at everything, and you can't go it alone. With that being said, you don't have to have years of experience to launch your expert business. You can begin with a few great clients who believe in you and then learn the rest from other experts as you grow. Not knowing how to do something has never held me back from launching a new business—and it shouldn't stop you either!

The RD&T Method

Look closely at every piece of marketing that comes your way and think about how you could make it work for *your* business. Ask yourself, "How and when can I implement that idea into my business, with a new twist to make it my own?" For example, I allow my clients to utilize the same systems they learned from working with me. I suggest that all of my clients create a pre-consulting questionnaire for their clients, just as I do. This helps them be more on target when they speak to their clients, and it sets them up for success. They can utilize my questionnaires and e-mails as a guide, but they must create something that works specifically for their business and their clients. Because it's not going to be exact, I have them use what I call the "RD&T Method": Research, Duplicate, & Tweak! Research your competition—see what they are doing, and go one better. Duplicate ideas and concepts, and put your own spin on it. This "tweak" part is extremely important for tailoring concepts and systems to fit your own unique needs.

There's no one original idea; you can take a concept and you can twist it a little bit to make it targeted toward your market. Every expert you work with should teach you systems that you can implement in your own business. For example, I once hired an expert for $5,000 just to get his questionnaire to use for my target market. Unfortunately, I didn't get many great ideas from this expert, but the questionnaire alone was worth my investment. It helped me to gain clarity and target my customers' needs even before we started to work together. Learning just one piece of a system I could implement into my own business was well worth the investment.

Staying Focused on Your Target Market

Your area of expertise has got to be narrowed down to a field with which you feel comfortable and with which you can also grow. Go deep into your subject matter and stay on course so that you don't offer something outside of your expertise.

To stay on target you must remain true to what you know and do best.

CHAPTER 9

STAKE YOUR CLAIM WITH ONLINE DOMINATION

THE INTERNET OFFERS YOU ONE OF THE FASTEST tools to develop and expand your expertise. Online, your opportunities are limitless. In the past, you would have to spend a lot of money on advertising and do a lot of face-to-face networking to get the word out about your business. Today, new businesses are launched or existing businesses are reinvented almost overnight online, and brand domination is key to getting noticed amid the chaos.

What is brand domination? Well, you have achieved brand domination when someone types your name or your brand name into a search engine online and the main expert they find on pages one, two, and three is you, your brand, and your expertise. There is no doubt about this; the search engines are considered to be all-powerful. They're the place where you can dominate with your brand and your expertise faster than ever before. I have two questions for you:

1. Have you ever typed in your name and really paid attention to what comes up?

2. Does your name and brand name show up on the first page of Google?

If the answer is yes to both of these questions, you are on your way to online domination. If the answer is no, you are missing out on attracting attract new clients online.

Why Brand Domination Is So Important

If you are the go-to expert in your marketplace, people want to know more about you before they meet or talk to you, and the Internet is the place where people go to find the answer to virtually any question they have. This means if someone wants to learn more about you, she is most likely going to turn to the Internet to check you out from a search engine. Of course, if she types in your name and cannot find you, the first thought that comes to her mind is simple: *Is this person really an expert in his field if Google hasn't listed him?* Yet, if you are listed high on Google, she will think you are the authority, because Google and other high-ranking search engines are listing you as the dominating person for that expertise. Let me put it this way: if you do not dominate, then someone else will! It's easy to search your competition online, and I suggest you do this in great detail. You need to know how to stand out from all of your competitors, so plan to spend some quality time online getting to know your competition and what they have to offer.

You must have Internet domination around your name and brand so that when people search for you online you can easily be found. This is the first step in determining what direction you'll take with your brand when building your expertise.

How Will People Search for You?

You need to gain Internet domination for both your personal name and your company's brand name. Why? If you are a well-known expert within your industry, people are more likely to search for you by your name than by your brand name. But if you have a brand name, and this is how you present your business or products to the marketplace, then you need to dominate for your brand name as well. People buy brands, so you want your brand name to be easy to remember. If you can dominate for your brand, you have achieved the first step toward online domination.

I am amazed at the number of businesses that fail to stand out because they have selected brand names that conflict with other businesses online. This will only set up roadblocks to getting more exposure online.

Choosing the Right Domain Name

The best place to begin your domination of the Internet is with your domain name—in other words, your Website name and address, such as TheHighlyPaidExpert.com, or JaneDoe.com. The domain name(s) you choose are key to your success. They must be easy to remember and rich with words that people often search for when seeking out an expert such as yourself. Search on one of the main search engines such as Google to see what other people are searching for around your brand and the services you offer. From there you will be able to find good phrases that could be utilized in additional domain names.

Also search for keyword-rich domain names that fit your expertise well and that will work around your corporate Website domain. By owning additional keyword domain names, you'll gain even more exposure and domination for your brand.

There are many places where you can search and buy domain names; one of the largest is GoDaddy.com, but many other companies sell domain names for less. I purchase most of my domains from GoDaddy simply because I like to keep all my domain purchases in one place. Because I have so many, it's hard to remember them all. For example, I have more than a dozen domain names focused on my expertise that simply point to my corporate Website, DebbieAllen.com. Therefore, whatever company you decide to buy your domains with, keep it consistent so that they all reside in one place.

Pay close attention to which domain name phrases are listed highest on the search engines when you do your keyword search. Also make a note of domain names that pay for advertising so that you don't have to compete with too many ads. On Google you can easily see ads highlighted at the top of the first page and down the right side of the page. If you can find a great domain name that is keyword-rich, is listed high on searches, and also doesn't have a lot of competition with advertisers, that's a great domain name to buy. Having less competition from advertisers will allow you to easily dominate the search engines.

Right now your opportunities to dominate online are still wide open on the worldwide Web. There are still plenty of great domain names available to you that will allow you to lead your brand. Recently I was able to grab some amazing domain names for some of my clients that I was surprised were still available online: StopDietingForLife.com, WealthBuildingForWomen.com, MoneyAndLifeFreedom.com, PassionToProfitsCoach.com, BookWritingSuccessCoach.com, and more. But be warned: You can't lead if you are going in the wrong direction. Buying a lot of the wrong domain name is simply a waste of time and money. Off-the-mark Web addresses won't give you the right traffic to your Website, and that's critical to gain exposure online and build your online database. I never brand any client until he can own the dot-com in many different formats around every part of his brand and expertise. If he can't own it, we switch the brand, change the business name, and go in another direction so that we can develop his domination once he launches or re-launches his business online.

Don't forget to grab the domain of your own name. For example, I've owned the domain DebbieAllen.com since 1995 (almost the Dark Ages of the Internet). Back then, I was just starting to build my expert business, and I understood the value of having my name out there as I grew my expertise. My name is a common name. In fact, there is a famous dance choreographer named Debbie Allen—I'm sure she wishes she owned my domain. If you do a search under that famous name, you'll find that we are both very Google-able. If you just put in "Debbie Allen" in your search, the other Debbie will be listed due to her massive celebrity following. Yet, I'm still showing up on page one due to the keyword domain name that I own. If you adjust the search slightly and put in "Debbie Allen Speaker," you'll notice that I dominate that search.

This is why owning domains with your name, plus keywords related to your expertise, is extremely important. Because I built my business around my name, it would not be smart to change it now. My name has become an important part of my brand (and it's also the only thing my ex-husband gave me that I want to keep).

Be sure you have your expert brand foundation in place (go back to Chapter 4 if need be) before buying any domain names, because if that's not aligned perfectly, the domain names and keywords you choose won't be consistent with your overall brand message. And anytime you put out mixed messages with your marketing, you lose out on business. For example, I was recently considering hiring a speaker whom I've known for years to speak at one of my upcoming events. Then, when I checked his Website and social media links, I discovered how disjointed his marketing was. Although this person is an amazing expert, I decided to take a pass and not ask him to speak.

Switching Brand Direction

What if you have one of those brand names that conflicts with other businesses online, or you need to go in a different direction to attract more clients? Do you close up shop? No! You switch your brand direction. When you really own your expert brand online, it's harder to switch to a new brand direction, but it can be done if you know how to redirect your online traffic. As long as you aren't going too far off your brand and market, you could shift things dramatically in a matter of months. For example, it was challenging for me to reinvent my business brand after leaving a three-year business partnership and a world tour when nearly 80 percent of my business was international. When I decided to leave the business partnership and get off the world tour, I had to rebuild my online brand, including my Website and social media accounts. It took a lot of work, but within a few months, I was able to completely redirect my brand and online domination. Once that happened, new and redirected opportunities began to appear.

Don't forget how important it is to set your brand name on a dot-com that you own. If you do need to, re-branding or create a new brand, make sure you do an online search first to see who is already listed with the same or a similar name.

Use Video to Promote Your Brand

After you have secured the dot-com domain name for your personal name and brand name, the next step is to create social media accounts for your name and/or brand name on Facebook, LinkedIn, Twitter, and Google+. Then you need to set up your own YouTube Channel. This is where you will add correctly optimized videos for more online exposure. You'll need to create quality content and publish it online with keyword-rich titles (see Chapter 12 for more on this). Selecting the correct titles for your videos is critical to getting listed high on search engines for the search areas in which you wish to be found.

Using video to promote your brand and Website is a key marketing tool for every expert, and using the right keywords in the video title you post online is extremely important to gain you more online domination. Google loves videos, so the videos you post online on YouTube can be listed high on a Google search in just a matter of days. The reason Google loves videos and ranks them high very quickly is that Google owns YouTube. Google purchased one of the other largest search engines (YouTube) for their own online domination back in 2006 for $1.6 billion.

There has never been a better time to claim your expertise and brand, so get out there and dominate your spot on the Internet.

Chapter 10

BUILD YOUR EXPERT WEBSITE

THE REASON MOST WEBSITES DON'T WORK effectively is that they have disjointed messages and/or too much information that confuses the viewer. You must remain consistent with your message and expertise throughout your Website. Often it's much easier to create a new Website than to modify an existing bad Website. This way, the site is completely aligned from the home page and navigates effectively to each additional page link.

Think about your Website as a smooth, wide path where you take viewers on a journey through your expertise, background, services, products, testimonials, credibility, and more. There are no obstacles along the path, and there are no confusing messages that send viewers in the wrong direction—just a simple and easy-to-follow, straightforward path. Nothing is disjointed or unclear; everything leads your viewer exactly where you want them to go, toward taking the action you want them to take.

Putting together a clearly defined Website is a skill from start to finish, and that's why having the right team to build it is critical to your success online. It's well worth the time and effort to develop a dynamic Website, because all of your online opportunities will flow there. Your credibility and expertise are at stake if you don't have a great Website that effectively markets you and your organization. If you are not getting the right clients or making the amount of money you deserve, I guarantee there is something going on with your Website that is blocking your opportunities.

When prospects check out your Website, they will take note of your marketing messages to see what makes you unique from other experts in your industry. They will notice your logo, your images, your video, your call to action, everything. They will make a quick decision based upon whether they want to read on, watch more videos, take action, or simply click away.

Today you can't just put your Website up and forget it; your Website needs to remain a work in progress. It takes constant tweaking, adjusting, editing, and adding. Your Website will never be complete. In fact, in today's market you'll need more than just one Website. Experts require more than one Website to get noticed online.

Consider having your main corporate site, landing page(s), event Website, blog, and more. Never stop improving your Websites and updating your expert image online.

Redefine, Reposition, and Re-Energize Your Online Opportunities

If you don't get your Website right, it could be costing you thousands, even millions, in lost opportunities. Here's an example, from my client Rick Benson, who has a custom home-building business. He had a Website that was launched in the late 1990s, but he never made it a priority to improve or update his site. In the meantime, he was busy out there working *in* his business, building word-of-mouth referrals, great service, and great quality. This helped build his more than 30-year-old construction company...until more and more people started going online to research everything before deciding to make a purchase.

Times had changed dramatically since Rick had first launched his Website. One day he discovered firsthand just how much his Website was keeping him from getting new business when one of his prospects decided to go in another direction after seeing Rick's outdated Website. Although Rick is an amazing builder, the image from his Website and brand didn't match his level of expertise, and that mistake cost him tens of thousands of dollars in lost business. And what makes it even worse is that he had no idea how much money had already been lost to other prospects that had judged his Website poorly at first glance. Many of them may have simply clicked away to one of his competitors whose expertise was clearly showcased online with a more effective Website. Rick had to learn this lesson the hard way before deciding to rebuild his brand and a new Website, now located at CastleGateCustomHomes.com.

Here's how you can redefine, reposition, and re-energize your online opportunities:

◆ **Redefine:** If you have an existing Website, take a look at all the text on your site. Make sure it is speaking directly to your target market. If not, rework your marketing copy altogether to get more effective results.

◆ **Reposition:** It may be time for you to completely reinvent your brand and/or marketing direction. If so, you'll need to create a new logo and brand message to reposition yourself in the marketplace.

◆ **Re-Energize:** If you have a good existing Website, you may be able to simply update each page. If your business has changed, you will need to build a completely new Website to re-energize your online presence.

Most Websites are now created in a simple WordPress format. Take the time to get your Website done right before it costs you dearly in lost sales, opportunities, and income.

7 Steps to Take Before Building or Rebuilding Your Website

Step 1: Get your brand foundation developed or redesigned

Schedule a professional photo shoot to get updated photos for your Website. I suggest you get some great headshot photos as well as some action shots to use throughout your Website. Bring a few changes of clothing to get multiple images. Also try to match the colors of your clothing to your overall brand.

Ask your Webmaster to begin your Website by first developing the banner and masthead. A masthead is a graphic image and/or text title at the top of a Webpage that identifies the Website. It's important that the masthead showcases the overall look, feel, and colors of your Website and background. Your banner is very important, because this is where your initial benefit message or unique selling proposition (USP) will go. Inside your banner, you'll also want to add your logo and photo or image. If you are the personal brand for your business, add an updated headshot photo of yourself with your tagline or credentials listed under it. If your company is the brand, add an image that best complements your logo and marketing message.

Step 2: Develop copy for your homepage

Write emotionally rich, benefit-driven copy for your site focused toward a specific target market. Begin with your homepage and then add additional pages. Creating great copy will be critical to your online success. When writing your marketing copy for your site, make sure to use words that speak directly to the ideal target market. Keep in mind that this is not about *you*, it's about the unique service you provide, the pain you relieve, and the solutions you offer that get results. Think about the outcome you achieved for your most satisfied client and write in those terms. Here is what you should include in your home page copy:

◆ A strong, benefit-rich title and a results-driven message that lead viewers to action.

◆ A few well-written paragraphs that describe the benefits of what you do and what makes you different from your competitors.

◆ Four to six bullet points that include the benefits and features of what you have to offer. These should be powerful offers that speak directly to your prospect; choose your marketing words carefully and wisely to attract the exact type of clients you wish to receive.

◆ Great testimonials from your raving fans. Be sure to add the full name of the client on the testimonial. Video testimonials are now becoming even more powerful marketing tools than the written word.

Step 3: Continue to write additional pages for your Website

Once your banner and home page copy has been completed, begin to add additional pages one by one. On a WordPress Website, the right side of your home page will feature two boxes. One box will show your FREE offer and the other box features your branding video. Try to keep these two boxes "above the fold" (easily viewed on the computer without scrolling down the page). Your additional Web page links may include these: About, Speaking, Media, Articles, Coaching or Consulting, Services, Events, Blog, Testimonials, and Contact.

Step 4: Use the right images

If images on your site are not professional, prospects may negatively judge the quality of your work at first glance. The same applies to having updated professional photos of yourself online. The image you present will set the tone for your overall business quality, so invest in quality images. A few resources where you can find good quality images for purchase are iStockPhoto.com, ShutterShock.com, and BigStockPhoto.com.

Step 5: Create a strong call to action

A clear, decisive call to action helps you generate sales and capture future customers. Your call to action must have a clear, explicit purpose. There's no harm in telling people what you want from them, such as "Call us for a quote," or "Contact us to learn more about our consulting services." If you want people to take action, you must guide them to the next step.

Step 6: Make your Website easy to navigate

Once visitors are on your Website, make sure they can easily find whatever it is they're looking for. If they can't find it easily, they will simply click away and are not likely to come back. Make sure you incorporate a clear navigation bar that takes viewers by the hand and walks them through your site. Also be careful not to add layers upon layers of sub-link categories in your navigation. Generally, only two layers of depth are recommended; otherwise it becomes too unfocused. That's the reason each Website you build needs to be simple and easy to navigate. For example, if you have many different services, you may want additional Websites for different divisions of your business.

Step 7: Include a sign-up form

A sign-up form helps you build a list of potential customers. Give your prospects a way to learn more about what you do, while you stay connected to them. Entice visitors to sign up by offering something of value (such as your free offer) in return for their contact information. Building a large database of followers is extremely important for building warm leads and prospects who are open to purchasing the products, books, and services you offer. You'll want to ask for first name (only) and e-mail address; asking for any additional information will dramatically cut down the number of viewers who sign up for your free offer. Make it easy for them to sign up.

Great Marketing Copy Is Critical to Your Online Success

Your Website must instantly connect and build credibility with people. The home page is where you should spend the most quality time working on crafting every word of your site that directly relates to your most ideal clients. Don't expect your Webmaster to create a Website for you with marketing copy that drives clients to you like crazy; it's just not going to happen. Your Website is only going to be as good as the content *you* provide. No matter how pretty or professional your Website may appear or how much money you paid for it, it's not going to be effective without great marketing copy.

Driving traffic to your Website is only important after you have an effective Website. If you are sending traffic to a bad site, no amount of traffic is going to help you get clients online. To develop great marketing copy that promotes your expertise effectively, you either need to be a great marketer yourself, or you need to hire a marketing expert who knows how to write great copy to help you out. It's a team effort to get it just right. Remember that your Website is the most powerful online marketing tool you can own—you don't want to leave it to chance. It must be done correctly to gain the type of Internet domination you wish to achieve around your brand and expertise.

You must make sure your copy is written in such a way that it speaks directly to your target market and leads them to action. Touch viewers' emotions and pain points, and offer real solutions within your text. Also make sure that the top third of your page (above the "fold" or screen shot) includes strong, attention-grabbing benefit messages. You want your viewers to quickly understand what you're all about and what benefits you are offering them at first glance. Otherwise they will simply click away.

At the bottom of your home page, create a good call to action statement to drive viewers to the next step—working with you. If you don't ask for action, no action will be taken.

Let Viewers Get to Know You

The next important item to add to your home page is an introduction video whereby viewers can personally connect to you as the expert. It should be no more than two minutes in length, as it's hard to keep your viewers' attention for much longer than that. Your video should welcome viewers to your site and showcase your personality. Relax, be yourself, and have fun with it. Start out by offering a benefit statement about your business. Next, offer a couple of tips, ask them to look around your site, and invite them to sign up for your free offer. Your main goal should be to make a personal connection and then give away a free gift so that viewers feel comfortable giving you their e-mail address. The more personalized you make your video, the more they will feel as though they already know you.

Allow viewers to get to know you on your "About" page. This is where you can brag about your expertise, background, media attention, and so on. Let viewers in by sharing something personal about you or something most people don't know about you to make it more interesting. For example, in the past, I didn't tell people that I had never attended a day of college or that I had never applied for a job in my life. I also failed to mention early on that I had little knowledge of any industry I launched into and was often under-capitalized when I began. None of these where great business models to follow. Therefore, early on in my expert career, I believed that if I told people those things, I would lose my credibility. But what I soon discovered was that my grass-roots way of marketing and my life-long entrepreneurial background were what I could use to set myself apart. I then began sharing my personal experiences and obstacles to my advantage. My stories of triumph over challenge now are a strong motivator for my audience and prospects with a "no rules" and "no excuse" attitude of approaching business.

Find your own unique story to make a strong connection and add a personal touch to your Website; people always enjoying reading stories. Your stories also make you more real and authentic to online prospects. This way your online marketing will build credibility and trust.

CHAPTER 11

DEVELOP A SOCIAL MEDIA STRATEGY

THE TWO QUESTIONS MOST PEOPLE ASK ABOUT social media are, "Where should I be?" and "What do I post?" With so many social media sites to consider (and more popping up all the time), selecting the right ones to put your marketing efforts into is important. You want to receive a good return on investment for your time and effort. To get the best and fastest returns, it's important to know what each social media site can offer you and how to best utilize each one. Each one has a different format and a different group of followers. That's why you must have a social media strategy in mind before jumping in.

When I first started using social media, it was really an experiment to see what kind of business opportunities I could find without spending too much of my marketing budget. Every time I went online, I was looking for opportunities to connect with the right followers without trying to sell something. I began building valuable relationships with people who could (a) become a strong joint venture partner, (b) hire me to speak, or (c) become a warm prospect. Soon my efforts started paying off, and within a couple of months, I had secured a few speaking engagements by directing my new connects to my Website via Facebook and LinkedIn.

Back in 2009, I received a speaking engagement in Dublin, Ireland, from Facebook. I noted on the organization's page that I was a great fit for their conference, and also saw that they had no female speakers on their platform. I used this to my advantage and softly promoted my expertise and Website. After a few connections back and forth on Facebook, the conference had booked me to speak. Around the same time, I was connecting with a possible joint venture partner: another female speaker who was speaking on large platforms around the world. I believed we had similar (but not competing) marketing skills and that we could refer one another to get on more stages. Once I got booked to speak at the event in Dublin, I referred my new JV (joint venture) partner, and she also got booked to speak. About three months later, we were both traveling together on the same flight from Los Angeles to

Dublin. While in Dublin, we met another female speaker. We were the only three women to speak at the conference. Instantly we felt a connection: each of us was an expert on different topics of marketing, including branding, the Internet, and media. We decided to join forces and do a speaking tour together, and *that* led to a three-year world tour of nearly 20 countries! This is just one example of the opportunities that have come my way by utilizing social media. So you can understand why I believe so strongly in having a social media strategy. It really pays off!

The time you spend on social media should have one main goal: to eventually get your social media followers to your Website. Once they take action and move to your Website, you can convert more followers into warm leads. As you gain experience with your own social media, you will be able to uncover what works and doesn't work for your business.

Turn Followers Into Warm Leads

Building a large social media following is important, but if you are not converting those followers to join your own database, they are not *your* followers. Social media is always changing, and that makes your social media following volatile. You could lose your following at any time because you don't "own" them. It's easy for people to "Like" you on Facebook, but those followers don't belong to your personal database. For example, if your social media site is hacked, you could actually lose all of your followers and will need to start all over again to rebuild your following.

This "hacking" nightmare happened to one of my clients: She had built a large database of more than 25,000 followers on her fan page, when someone got into her Facebook page and hacked all of her followers in one day. This didn't just happen once, but twice! What was even more devastating was that she believed she had a huge following, but since she had not moved them over to her Website to convert them to her e-mail list, she was actually not building a database. Building your own database is key to developing a real online following. Once you turn followers into warm prospects, you can market to them at any time: you can promote your expertise via a newsletter, where you can also talk about your services, products, and events.

Once you get followers to sign up on your Website, you'll want to have a "call to action." Again, this is where your free offer comes into play. Let's say your free offer is a guidebook. Your guidebook can be a 10- to 15-page list of tips with an enticing call to action at the bottom. A strong call to action will lead warm prospects to the next step. For example, your action step may be to ask them to sign up for a free coaching call or to invite them to attend a free online class. This is a great opportunity for you to convert warm leads into buyers.

Convert Followers Into Real Fans

Once followers start receiving valuable free information from you, they turn into *real* fans that follow your social media posts, newsletters, blogs, and more. When your free sign-up is tied into e-mail auto-responders, you develop an automated system that does the marketing for you. For example, let's say you have a Facebook follower who is directed to your Website for your offer. Once on your Website, she learns more about your expertise and enters her e-mail address—now she is in your database. This is why it's so important to have a great Website with all the right bells and whistles set up before social media can do the work for you.

Most social media followers will "opt in" to your free offer right away to learn more from your expertise. Your offer must be something of high value to keep their interest. Followers won't sign up for just a newsletter—who needs another one of those? What followers *do* need is information they can implement right away. They need your expert advice. For example, my client Shelley Gillespie is the "Book-Writing Success Coach." She offers a free guidebook called "10 Steps to Book-Writing Success." And that's exactly what her ideal prospect is looking for—instant information and valuable tips on how to write a book. Because Shelley gives good value up front, viewers feel comfortable offering their e-mail addresses in exchange for her information.

Look at social media as a tool to turn "cool" fans into "warm" prospects. Then, with your auto-responder marketing, you can begin to turn more prospects into buyers. Of course, they can always "opt out" of your database at any time, but if they do, they were not true followers anyway. The quality of your database following can become even more important than the number of followers you have. You want to build a quality database with followers who have come to respect your expertise and want to keep learning more from you.

Measure the Return on Your Investment

The question of measuring your social media marketing return in exchange for time can be a tricky one. Can you really say whether a certain customer came to you because of a particular social media post, or was it a result of several different marketing activities? When utilized strategically, social media can help market your business, but you must put some type of measurement on your return. Merely having a social media presence is not your objective—it's much more than that. To track your results, you must find a way to track whether the people you are engaging with on social media are turning into warm leads and, eventually, customers.

All social media sites have some kind of analytical data you can pull from them. Facebook and LinkedIn both have "insight," and Twitter and YouTube have "analytics." In each case, the data is helpful to give you demographics and the level of engagement you are achieving. But you'll really see the results when your posts and connections are strategically placed. This is why it's so important to use social media as a tool for driving people back to your Website. Your Website is the only place online where you have 100-percent control over how your brand and expertise is showcased. It is also the place where you can gather the most information about your market.

Great content is the secret to keeping fans. You must have plenty of content on your Website, including helpful tips, expert strategies, and answers to the questions many of your prospects have. You must teach instead of making it a sales pitch, especially on your homepage. Let followers get to know you first. Your follow-up e-mails and ongoing marketing will sell them on you over time.

Which Social Media Sites to Pay Attention To

So, let's go back to the initial question, "What social media sites should I be on?"

The answer is: You should be on the sites that get you the best results from the content you are promoting. What sites are driving the most traffic to your Website?

Although I have received great value from Facebook, my most effective social media site today is LinkedIn, because it drives the bulk of the social media traffic to my Websites and my events. It is a virtual powerhouse of strong lead generation, largely due to postings in targeted LinkedIn groups. The reason it's such a great social media site for targeting is that it is largely a professional audience. LinkedIn groups generate fast leads and warm prospects to my specific target market. I use it to promote to groups that have business owners who can directly benefit from my expertise. I've converted a countless number of "cool" leads to "hot" buyers, generating thousands of dollars in return by making connections within these groups.

Connections you make on social media allow you to continually grow your database with new prospects and more buyers. This can also be done using Facebook ads. Consider what social media search engine sites will be best for your business and your promotions.

One of the most misunderstood social media networks is Twitter. It forces users to condense their message into a brief 140 characters, and the result is a massive amount of information to work through. You may be a bit of a skeptic when it comes to how Twitter will help you grow your business, but it's working for many experts. It is useful as long as what you are posting is driving traffic back to your Website to generate leads.

Always keep in mind that the goal of social media is to convert visitors into leads. If your social media is not converting viewers, you probably have the same problems everyone else who isn't making money online has: either you aren't posting great content or your Website isn't converting due to poor marketing copy. Another reason you may not be converting visitors into leads could be that you are either marketing to the wrong niche market or targeting too general of an audience. The truth is that your presence on social media will work when you post great content to the right market that leads to effective Website copy. You can't skip a step and expect it to work effectively; it just doesn't happen that way. There are no shortcuts. All of your online marketing and branding must be on target and focused to create feedback and action. For example, if all you did was post inspiring quotes or pretty photos, you might build a following, but you wouldn't get qualified leads. Without warm leads, you can't measure your impact in a way that is meaningful to your social media objectives.

Don't worry about whether you are on *all* the social media platforms. Just get your business signed up for some of the most important social media search engines, such as Facebook, LinkedIn, Twitter, and Google+. Use the same business name on all of the sites if possible. Keep your branding consistent on all of them to promote your expertise effectively.

Be Share-Worthy

Keep in mind that social media is all about sharing—you need to give people something "share-worthy" in order to make your social media marketing strategy work for you. One thing you can do is add photos and images for impact, because a picture is truly worth a thousand words in social media. There is a lot of text on social media, so using your own great-looking images and quotes can help you stand out from the crowd, as long as they are posted in a way that leads them back to your site. When you post an original photo or quote, your comments and Likes should go up dramatically.

Using your own quotes is a great way of developing a strong expert following. One great resource to help you create an image for your quotes is Quozio.com. This site is easy and free to use. You simply post your original quote and your name. But instead of just posting your name, also post your Website, because your quotes will also get followers to your Website. Select an image to go with the quote, and then download the whole image. It's that easy! Create a number of personalized quotes and images, save the files to post periodically on your social media sites, and watch the comments and shares pile up.

Educate and Inform With Your Expertise

Today's online followers want to be informed; they don't want to be sold to or spammed with constant promotions. That's a fast way to lose followers and fans on social media. Use your social media posts for brief, interesting information, links to relevant blog posts, or your expert articles. You can also link to case studies, client testimonials, updates about your company, expert content, contests, videos, and more. Cartoons and funny images can also be good as long as you keep your brand and expertise intact. Laughter is both contagious and memorable, so injecting some humor into your social media can be a great way to show off your personality and make your followers feel more comfortable engaging with you.

Select a theme to show some fun photos and videos for upcoming events or new content you've added to your Website. Fun images always gain attention and help you to stand out. For example, when I promoted my event in Las Vegas, I used photos of me with a showgirl, or with props and signs I've found in casinos. And when I've done events in Hollywood I've featured fun photos with big Hollywood-themed glasses or a movie clipboard. You must find ways to have fun and engage online followers.

Create personal connections. After all, that's the primary goal of "social" networks—to be social! Make sure that some of your content is thanking your followers for sharing, responding to comments and questions, and reposting or mentioning relevant content from your fan base.

Each Social Media Community Is Unique

Before you start posting to any social media sites, you should take some time to understand the expectations of its current users. Social media communities are all different, and each of the popular social media sites has its own unique community with distinct differences. For example, Facebook and Twitter are very different from Google+ and LinkedIn; they don't all communicate the same way. Twitter users, for example, don't mind seeing your posts several times throughout the day. Twitter streams are so fast that you can miss most of the updates unless you are posting something that is happening at that moment. For example, at each of my events we ask the audience to post what they are learning and experiencing during the live events with a hashtag (#) so that viewers can see instant interaction.

If you want to stay relevant on Facebook, you don't want to post too much. Typically one or two posts per day can be enough to keep you relevant there. LinkedIn followers, on the other hand, are often too busy to constantly post to their profiles (although I normally post five or six times a week on LinkedIn because my groups are so targeted). Join targeted groups first, and your investment of time in conversations in these groups will pay off.

Social media is a moving target that is quickly evolving. With Google+, you have the opportunity to both create and effectively track how well your content is getting engagement. The key is trying different things until you see what works. Followers on Google+ join circles (or groups) and like hanging out. When your content is shared here, you will often find it has the greatest reach, and may even have some content going viral. One of the greatest tools that Google+ offers is its hangout video format, making it "the new mix" between YouTube and Facebook. The popularity and growth of this social media site is something to pay close attention to. Once you discover where you get the best return for your time and effort, you'll begin to develop a social media strategy that works best for your business.

CHAPTER 12

CREATE ONLINE DOMINATION WITH VIDEO MARKETING

MARKETING, ESPECIALLY ONLINE MARKETING, continues to change. As an expert, you want to know where it's all heading and how you can stay on top of it. When it comes to getting the edge on your competition and becoming *the* online authority, video is where it's at. And as an expert, you already have a special advantage in working with videos to dominate your expertise online because you really know your stuff! Your goal is to create quality content based on your expertise, and get out as much good video as possible to gain authority domination online.

Why Video Works

In the simplest terms, the memory portion of our brain works in a three-step process: sensory memory, short-term memory, and long-term memory. This means that if you want a prospect to remember your brand and your expertise, your brand and your message need to be repeated. The more they are repeated, the better chance they have of getting stuck in the viewer's long-term memory. So you want to make your message stick, and videos are a great way to do this.

Videos help your brand and expertise by allowing you to dominate as an online authority. Videos have legs and are a great branding tool; they are one of the most powerful ways to quickly expand your expert brand and gain exposure. One of the first things a viewer is going to click on when they hit your Website or open your e-mail is a video. In fact, the main reason video marketing is so powerful is that most people say they'd be more likely to seek out information about a product or service after seeing it showcased in an online video.

Here are some more great benefits of videos:

◆ Having a video on your Website makes it 50 percent more likely to show up on page 1 of Google.

◆ Video marketing can dramatically help to increase click-through rates on e-mail marketing.

◆ Videos create higher viewer retention; the information retained in one minute of online video is equal to about 1.8 million written words.

◆ All business-to-business marketers use some form of online videos with their overall social media strategy.

It's hard to believe one marketing medium can transcend all industries' differences, but video marketing is it. Videos can yield great results, no matter what kind of service or product you are selling. It is imperative that, as an expert, you are creating videos to promote your expertise, because they will get watched and you will get noticed. The value that videos produce makes them well worth the time and investment.

Video marketing offers a high level of entertainment that can replace or supplement otherwise dry informational text. A good video can quickly grab a viewer's attention in a way that no other media can offer. A short and to-the-point video, approximately two minutes long, will keep the viewers' attention and can quickly tell your story. A well-produced video can profile an expert's products, service, and expertise in a visually compelling way, drawing more business opportunities and online exposure on many levels.

Stand Out Online With Keyword-Rich Videos

It used to be that businesses steered away from video production due to its exorbitant costs. Today, even small business owners on a modest budget can access the world of video by utilizing the power of video marketing on YouTube. If you don't already have a YouTube channel, make sure you create one, with a name that is directly related to your industry, business, or brand name (within YouTube's 30-character limit). If you have ever wished there was a way to land on the first page of search results that didn't involve the back-breaking work of traditional search-engine optimization, this is it. To get a great return from this strategy, be sure to also select the right titles for your videos so you have a better shot at getting listed on the first page of Google. Studies have shown that videos are more than 50 times more likely to appear on the first page of search engines when they have the right keywords in the title, description, and tags. The keywords you use in your video title should be based on the terms people are using to search for expertise in your field. Here are some very specific steps to follow to make this work.

First, upload your videos directly to YouTube. This won't necessarily guarantee you first-page results, but you can be certain that Google will index your video if it's uploaded there. Almost all the videos that Google shows on its searches are from YouTube. But this drives traffic to your YouTube channel, not your Website. That's why it's important to add your Website address and a call to action in the YouTube description box.

After adding your videos to YouTube, you may also want to embed them onto your Website, because it helps you get even more traffic and views. This is important because Google algorithms want to know how many times a video on YouTube has been watched. To help search engines like Google get a better understanding of what your content is all about, make sure you add a title introduction to the video that goes before the embedded video.

Your video will be found based on your title. Your title is what Google is most interested in when it comes to the term that is being used for a search. In other words, the title and search term must match your video title. The title influences the search rankings as well as the description and tags, so make sure you fill those in as well. Be sure that your video title and descriptions match the keywords you want to rank in.

Here's an example of how it all works. Let's use my client, Laura Fulford, The Christian Community Weight Loss Coach. Laura has a specialty niche market: she has created a proven weight-loss system designed specifically for the Christian Community. Her StopDietingForLife.com program is a faith-based approach to weight loss. This is a very narrow niche, yet a huge market (no pun intended). For Laura's video to dominate on a Google search, she would first need to post and edit her video on YouTube. Once the video is uploaded, she would add her title. This title would be no more than five keywords that best describe her expertise, such as "Christian Weight-Loss Program."

The next step Laura would take would be to complete the description box below the YouTube video. This is where she would repeat the title, using the exact same words, and would then add a more detailed description of the video and/or her expertise (just a couple of sentences), along with her Website address.

Below the description box is where she would post the tags. These tags are words that also help describe the video. Tags give the video a better chance of turning up on search engines. You want to make sure you don't go overboard with the tags here; simply use the same keywords you used in the title. For example, Laura would break down her title in the tag line area this way: Christian Weight-Loss Program, Christian Weight Loss, Weight Loss, Christian.

You can use this same approach to dominate the search engines for your specialty. You must also keep your marketing strategy in mind to discover the best keyword phrases that will gain you the best results.

Beyond YouTube

After you have posted your videos to YouTube it's easy to share them on Facebook, Twitter, LinkedIn, and Google+. Simply click the "Share" buttons for these sites when you post your video on YouTube.

Viral Marketing Expands Your Online Domination

Viral video marketing happens when your video gets shared over and over again. A good example of this is the social experiment created with Mentos and Diet Coke. This is one of the earliest records of a backyard experiment in which an entertainment science show turned a video into a cultural phenomenon. Unfortunately, at the time it was released, they missed a good opportunity to capitalize on the marketing when it was hot. You must learn how to use your expert ideas, strategies, and tips to capitalize on "hot" social media topics and make your viral marketing pay off. One of the biggest factors in social media marketing is the ability to act instantly to get real-time responsiveness. An increasing number of experts are learning to respond to breaking news with real-time information and commentary, all in video.

Location and Planning

In order to get high-quality videos out on social media in a timely fashion, it's important to have a production location already in place. Think about where you will be shooting: Will it be in your office, at home, or on location (indoors or outdoors)? Your location determines the type of camcorder, microphone, lighting, and backdrop you choose. For example, I have a basic video studio set up outside my office that includes a white muslin backdrop, a camcorder, and lighting stands. It's set up and ready to go anytime I'm inspired to shoot a video related to my marketing projects. If you don't have the space to set up your own video studio just yet, plan on shooting most of your video at a hotel or event location. Simply seek out the best lighting to avoid shadows on your face. Shoot up close and make your face the main focus of the video; this blocks out most of the background. Make sure to avoid shooting your video near signs, elevators, and doorways, because they can distract the viewer. Find a blank wall in a quiet area with good natural lighting.

If you choose a high-energy location where there are lots of people around, make sure that the right microphone is in place so the background noise doesn't drown out your voice. This is especially important when shooting video testimonials. Imagine getting a "raving fan" testimonial from one of your best clients, only to find out later the quality was too poor to use it. You may never have another chance to get a priceless video testimonial like that again. I've learned this lesson the hard way more than once.

To provide regular content for your videos, you need a shoot plan; this should be part of your overall marketing plan. I recommend a shoot plan that you can commit to for a minimum of three months. Think about what events, projects, promotions, topics, or ideas you can create videos about in this period of time. To be consistent with your video shoots you must commit to developing them on a regular basis. When committing to any video project, you should allow yourself a few tests before any big project. You'll likely find that more than just a few minor adjustments or "takes" will be required to give you the best video quality.

Learn How to Get Good on Video

Even after I had appeared in front of the camera for years, including in four motivational movies, I still didn't feel 100-percent comfortable on video. Speaking on video is a completely different format than speaking in front of people; it takes a different skill set. As an expert you *must* learn how to get good on video, because it provides way too much opportunity for you to ignore! Knowing this, I wanted to improve my skills and feel more comfortable shooting my own videos, so what I did was hire one of the best video experts in the business! Barbara Niven has been an actress in Hollywood for more than two decades, and she now utilizes her skills and expertise as an actress to help business owners, speakers, authors, salespeople, and other experts create high-quality videos that best show-case their authentic self. After spending a few days with Barbara at her Hollywood studio, I learned how to become a video pro. She taught me how to have fun with it and be myself—only better. If you want to learn how to sound great on camera and/or set up your own Google Hangout TV show, I highly recommend Barbara's video coaching and workshops at UnleashYourStarPower.com.

Use Video to Promote Yourself as an Expert Who Speaks

If you're making videos to promote yourself as a speaker, you must have live demo videos on your Website and your YouTube channel. Add a keyword title to each video so that you gain more online exposure and get your video listed high on the search engines fast. It's hard to keep someone's attention for a long time online, so keep your demo videos (or samples of your best presentations) short. Your demo video should offer quick tips showcasing your talents as a presenter, and it should be less than two minutes in length. If you have a long video of a good presentation, break it down into numerous talking points and short video clips. This will expand your online domination and ensure that your videos get watched in their entirety.

Keep adding and improving your demo videos all the time. Demo videos with great quality and great content will dramatically improve your chances of getting booked to speak.

To really make an impact with social media viewers on all platforms, being authentic on video is extremely important. Allow your followers to interact. Ask for feedback on your YouTube channel and allow prospects to submit their own questions, comments, or suggestions to your videos.

When you get it right, you'll see your videos quickly move up the ranks on Google and gain you a lot more traffic to your YouTube page and eventually your Website. Then you can sit back and watch your online authority domination soar.

CHAPTER 13

BIG-MONEY COACHING

COACHING IS A WONDERFUL CAREER THAT ALLOWS you to help others by helping them to become more accountable, learn new skills, overcome obstacles, inspire hope, and empower change. Much of the work of a coach is setting goals and then encouraging clients to achieve and exceed them. Coaches hold their clients accountable for their actions, and, for the coached, having someone hold you accountable can be life-changing. For the coach, seeing the change and growth in others is rewarding—that's what fills a coach's heart. Some coaches enjoy giving so much that they can actually give away too much and undervalue their services. Some even give away their coaching time freely, but giving away too much won't pay the bills. Once you learn here how to quickly communicate your value, how to develop more high-value coaching programs, and how to ask for more money, you'll be well on your way to becoming a highly paid coach.

Experts who coach are good at asking the right questions and being patient enough to listen, respond, direct, redirect, and hold their clients accountable to take action. A good coach is a caring and empathetic individual who enjoys making a difference in others' lives. Basically, when you think of a coach, you think of someone who guides you along the way. Coaches show you the shortcuts to getting the results you desire. They also help people find more effective ways to improve their businesses or their personal lives. People pay for coaches because they help them to solve problems faster, get them to a solution faster, and/or help them to make important decisions.

As an expert who coaches others, you must know the right questions to ask. You have to be a pretty good interviewer. If you think you're good at interviewing people and that you're patient enough to be a good listener, coaching may be right for you. A good coach gives his clients direct yet supportive responses. He communicates in a manner that gets others to listen and open up, and when he directs his clients to take action, they actually start moving. His clients start taking action because they feel that their coach has given them a direction that they can easily trust.

There are coaches for just about everything you could imagine. We used to think of a coach as someone who just coaches a sports team to win the game. Winning is their ultimate goal. Similarly, the ultimate goal for business and life coaches is to achieve a personal or professional win. Coaches help others win by helping them to achieve more success, achieve goals, relieve stress, and break through obstacles. There are coaches for family support, dating and marriage, addiction, and just about everything else you can imagine. I've worked with coaches for goal achievement, career development, career transition, personal empowerment, color therapy, personal healing, weight loss, and more. Other coaches I've worked with focus on specific industries and expertise such as accounting, carpet cleaning, and real estate.

Personally I have mentored many different types of business and life coaches in diverse industries. What I've discovered is that they have the same goal in mind: to improve their marketing so they can get more clients and make more money.

How to Start an Expert Coaching Business

What if you want to be a coach but don't know what direction to take or where to go? Having an interest and a passion is a good place to start. That's how many coaches start out: teaching what they most need to learn, because it's what interests them. For example, I had a client who had no idea what direction she was going to take when we started working together. All she knew was that she wanted to help people. So I said, "It's great that you want to help people, but what are you good at?" She responded, "I'm really good at procrastinating!" I laughed and said, "Okay, well then, should we move a little faster on this?!" She replied, "I sure know how to make excuses. I don't know if I can help others with that, but it's what I'm really good at. In fact, I'm so good at procrastinating that it's actually caused me a lot of pain. At times it has even made me feel bad about myself. I've found every excuse in the book when it comes to procrastinating."

"Are you still working through it?" I asked. She responded with, "Yes, it's always a challenge, but I've turned the corner. That's why I want to help people with the steps I've gone through to make the shift. I'm a different person now that I've I decided to take action." I said, "Great! There are a lot of people you could help take action, because most of us procrastinate to some degree. You can help others move past procrastination and lead them to more productive lives. That can be really life-changing for a lot of people."

Once we decided this was the direction we wanted to take her business and brand we came up with the name "The Stop Procrastination Coach." "Do you think there are a lot of people who procrastinate?" I asked her. "Do you think you have a market for that, and can you teach a course on this?" Of course she agreed it would be a large market, and she was excited to begin a speaking career around her expertise as well. She then began teaching what she most needed to keep learning. Because she had already gone through the pain and the challenges that procrastination brought her, she also understood how to move away from it and how to help others do the same.

She quickly started getting speaking presentations where she would sell her coaching programs. I was in an audience with her at one of her presentations and was amazed how good a speaker she was right out of the gate. She was real, engaging, and funny! She had a down-to-earth personality that instantly drew people in. She had a natural sense of humor and used her own personal stories and some fun self-deprecating humor to make her points during the presentation.

At the beginning of our work together, my client had no idea what she would teach and coach others on, but it was right there in front of her from her own life lessons. Similarly, you don't need to have a background as a therapist or counselor to be a coach. For example, many life coaches have backgrounds as successful businesspeople, entrepreneurs, educators, human resource administrators, psychiatrists, psychologists, social workers, or counselors. Many turn to life coaching because of the opportunity to help people who are already functioning well function even better.

You can get training as a coach, but it's not required. I do suggest that you work with a coach, consultant, or another expert so you can learn how to incorporate their coaching systems into your own coaching business. Or, if wish to get accredited, you can check out International Coach Federation or the International Association of

Coaching. But what is most important is that you give your clients real value and stick to a professional code of ethics as you work with them.

Pick a Path and Lead With Your Heart

Here are five questions to ask yourself when defining your coaching business:

1. What skills do you have that you can coach others on?

2. What support can you offer to help others overcome personal or professional obstacles that prevent them from achieving their goals?

3. What is your background and how can you use what you've learned to help others?

4. What credibility have you achieved or awards have you received from past experiences?

5. In what areas can you help others to cut their learning curve?

Decide what path you want to take with your coaching business and *own* it. For example, you can't call yourself a "business and life coach." You're either going to be a personal life coach or you're going to be a business coach—one or the other, not both! People often need to work with a life coach first to get their personal matters in order before working with a business coach. Both are equally important—which one fits you best? Select just one direction to follow or you'll come across as too generalized.

Life coaches are professionals who work with people to help them build on their past successes and make desired changes in their personal life. A business coach is a little different. A business coach focuses strictly on the business aspect of the coaching. So again, I suggest you don't mix the two, because what will happen is that you will dilute your brand. It will cause you to lose your entire brand message, and people are going to say, "What are you good at? Are you better at life coaching or are you better at business coaching?" You can't do both, so pick a path.

Share Your Passion and Enthusiasm

Make a list of everything you're personally enthusiastic about, things that you can really share your passion for to the point that you bring your heart into the service. When you share your passion for what you teach, you are authentic and always come from the right place.

Your work will always feel more like play when you teach what you love.

You must be passionate about helping other people; it has to come from your heart. Some highly paid coaches just look at is as a business and focus mainly on the money. Yet, I believe that if you're going to be good at something and really make a difference in others' lives, you *must* come from a place that touches your heart. When you connect your head (wisdom) with your heart (passion), you will begin to make a difference and see more personal shifts with your clients. When your clients experience this type of transformation, they will become your raving fans and your referrals will soar.

Set Yourself Apart From the Masses

There are a lot of life and business coaches. How will you set yourself apart from the Sea of Sameness and define your expertise? You must find an area where you can dominate in the marketplace. When you pick a clear path to follow, the right opportunities and clients will come your way because they will clearly understand your brand and admire your wisdom and expertise.

After you pick your direction, you'll need to break it down even more to become specialized. For example, I have a couple of clients who are life coaches who specialize in the area of life purpose. My client Nadia Tumas has branded herself The Life Purpose Decoder and Suzanne Strisower has branded herself as Awaken to Your Life Purpose. Not only did they each pick a specific path to follow, they branded their expertise within a highly competitive niche market of life coaching and life purpose.

Join Forces With Your Competition

Discover ways to go deeper into your chosen field of expertise and narrow it down to a very specific niche that you can be known for. Then collaborate with other experts to expand your database. When you find other experts who do similar work, offer to joint venture with them to create more opportunities for both of you. You can do joint venture teleseminars, Webinars, live events, book projects, expert interviews, and more. It can be a great win/win with the right joint venture partners. Your competitors can be your best form of marketing because you both have the same target market to focus on.

Get to know what your competition is all about. What are they doing that works, and what are they doing that is different from your approach? Knowing your competition well help you to define your own uniqueness. It helps you to fill holes in the same market.

Never Undervalue Your Services

Coaching is an awesome business to be in: you can set your own schedule, you get paid well for doing it, and you can work the way you want around your lifestyle. It's also an easy business to get into, actually. But the main problem many coaches have is that they undervalue themselves and charge low hourly fees. Charging by the hour will keep you stuck and broke in the coaching business. So let me say it like this: "No more charging dollars per hour!" Unless you are charging fees of $5,000 an hour or more, charging by the hour is not the way to go. To move from dollar-per-hour to a highly paid coach, you must learn how to effectively communicate the value you offer and how to sell it effectively.

When you deliver the best results, you can charge more because prospects see your value. People pay for results, solutions, guidance, and accountability. They pay for the final outcome of your work, so think about how you can tell others what you do in the form of outcomes. For example, share case studies about your clients who showed amazing results from working with you. Share stories of how you took your clients step by step through your systemized coaching process and helped them achieve their goals. People love to hear the success stories you have to share. Success stories and client testimonials help you sell your services. In fact, charging by the hour can actually be harder to sell than higher-priced bulk packages because you are always selling your clients into more time with you and undervaluing your expertise.

Build More Value by Creating Coaching Packages

Break down your coaching services into packages that include your services along with personal coaching, e-mail access, group calls, a product, and so on. Package your programs into monthly programs anywhere from one month to a full year and avoid the dreaded "dollar-per-hour keeps you broke" cycle.

Name your coaching packages based upon what you specialize in. For example, my two-month program is called a "Jumpstart Business Accelerator" and my extended five-month program is called "Highly Paid Expert Program." Use titles that relate to your services and your expertise.

Create two or three levels at different price points. The best investment and the best value for your prospect would always be your largest coaching package. Your pricing would depend on your level of expertise, the number of prospects you currently have, what type of coaching you do, along with what the market will pay for your services. This is going to be different for every coach. For example, you may offer a one-month program for $2,500, a three-month program for $4,500, and a six-month program for $7,500. Of course, the best value here is the six-month program. The whole idea is to move your buyer up to the higher-priced program that gives more value and more time with you. Everyone wins here: you get more income up front and clients gain more value from working with you for an extended period of time.

Once you finalize your coaching program details, post them on your Website along with your pricing. You'll want to have pricing on your Website so that prospects can get a sense of what level your programs are at. This applies to coaching programs *only* (not speaking fees). I also suggest you list your prices a bit higher on your Website than you would if you made a "special value" offer at a speaking engagement. For example, if your three-month coaching program sells for $4,500 on your Website, you may want to make a special offer for quick action-takers who pay in full at a live event for $3,997. Adjust your pricing and your programs as your business and client base grows. It's always a good day when you can give yourself a raise!

CHAPTER 14

HIGHLY PAID CONSULTING

IF YOU ARE CONSIDERING ADDING COACHING or consulting to your expert services, you'll need to know the difference between the two. Understanding this will help you to pick a path and a title that best describes your type of service. The difference between coaching and consulting is that coaching focuses on helping an individual clarify and work toward achieving a goal, whereas consulting involves providing expertise, analysis, and recommendations for how an organization can solve a specific problem. Consulting is usually very tactically oriented.

Mentoring is similar to consulting, but it's normally done by someone who has decades of experience behind her in a specific skill and/or industry. Coaches, consultants, and mentors all involve a skilled professional who assists a client in achieving his or her goals; the only differences lie in how the professional supports the client.

A coach usually works one on one with a client to facilitate personal or professional change. The coach listens, asks questions, and holds the client accountable. A coach helps clients create success by focusing on personal development: time management, self-sabotaging behavior, finding clarity, decision making, and getting into action. Coaches don't normally give advice; instead they help clients find the answers from within themselves.

A consultant (or mentor) works with clients on strategy, planning, and problem solving, and helps clients develop skills and knowledge by offering advice. Topics are normally business related, including designing a business model or marketing plan, developing a team, and determining which techniques to use and how to use them.

You can call yourself a coach, consultant, advisor, or mentor, and most clients will understand that it means you'll help them solve problems and grow, either personally or professionally. Consultants take on more of a guiding role and advise their clients to do the work that will achieve the results they desire. If you believe you are not the "hand-holding" type and are more of the "advisor" type, then consulting may be a better fit for you than coaching.

Four Steps to Building Your Consulting Business

Step 1: Solve problems. Become a problem-solver for your clients.

Step 2: Offer a promise. Create programs that can best serve your clients' needs.

Step 3: Show proof. Use testimonials and case studies that state your clients' results.

Step 4: Create a proposal. Set up your program and service offerings in detail.

Consultants Ease the Pain

A lot of people are in pain in their personal lives or in their businesses in some way. Experts such as yourself help them find the solutions to solve the problems and eliminate the pain. Figure out ways to solve problems for people and communicate this in your marketing copy. For example, let's say you have a client who is stuck in his business and he just can't figure things out on his own anymore. Let's say that he used to make a lot of money, but now his business has dropped off and he is losing clients and income. Ouch; this is painful! As a business consultant you can help him figure out where the problems are and advise him to change something to turn his business around. Once you help him turn his business around with the steps you suggest, his pains and frustrations begin to go away. You then become his business savor!

And that's why he'll pay you the BIG BUCKS!

From your very first meeting or call with a client, you give her hope. This instantly helps build her confidence like never before, and when you can do this for her, it's powerful! She can't wait to talk to you the next time and continue working with you. Usually the only pain my clients have at the end of my programs is that they don't want to let me go. When this happens to you, you'll know that you have provided results and a successful lifeline for your clients to hold on to. When people consider your expertise and advice as their lifeline, that's when your consulting business really takes off. You know you're on the right track when you get to work with ideal clients who trust your expertise and pay you well for your services. That's where the highly paid coach or consultant aspires to be.

Set Yourself Up for Success

How you approach a client is important when it comes to how you will work with him, either as a coach or a consultant. For example, I have a systemized step-by-step program that guides my clients through a business and brand strategy that is tailored specifically to them. I advise my clients with a very direct, honest approach. Clients must be coachable and open to getting results from my advice because we work quickly and effectively. Your ideal clients should not only be ready for change, but they must also be ready to take action so that you both achieve success in the process. Understanding who your ideal client is and how you want to work with him is very important to enjoying a thriving expert business. This is why you must communicate to your clients up front in a way that best serves you both as a team. Your clients must resonate with who you are and how you do business. They are going to respect who you are and how you do business before they decide to come onboard to work with you.

To be successful as a coach or consultant, you must get the right type of clients—those who take action. If your clients are not taking consistent action to change, you can't get them successful results. You only want to take on clients to whom you can offer 100-percent guaranteed results. This sets you both up for success! When you get a prospect who wants to become a client, make sure you ask her if she is ready to take action and change something in her life or business. Remember that your clients *must be coachable*. If not, they could become a nightmare to work with.

Coaching, consulting, and mentoring are all done at a personal level. You get to know your clients well and build trusted relationships. Personally, I get to know my clients so well that they become part of what I call my Business Family. This more personalized approach works well for me because I love building and growing companies. I enjoy getting personally involved with my clients' change and growth. Yet I also have a team of experts who work with me to do the technical aspects, graphics, and Website development for my clients. My consulting time is spent on personal guidance, direction, motivation, and ongoing business support; the rest is delegated to my team. The lesson is, know what you do best and delegate the rest. Work together as a team. Be clear about how you want to share your personal time with clients, and remember that your personal time is your biggest asset and the most valuable part of your services.

Systemize the Process

This is one area that can be time-consuming to figure out and set up at first, but once you have a proven system in place, your consulting program will run like clockwork and you'll be able to take on more clients and monetize your consulting programs more effectively. Every part of your consulting program must be systemized, including your client follow-up e-mails. Be sure to follow up with a new client within 24 hours of signing up with your program. Assure him that he made the right choice to work with you with a personalized e-mail and/or video.

Develop a client follow-up plan. Write e-mails in advance and create a pre-program questionnaire to help guide your support before you begin working with new clients. It took me a long time to develop a well-oiled program that had a step-by-step process that worked for all my consulting programs. It takes time to test and adjust until you have it down to a science, but once you have a system in place, you'll be able to work faster and more productively.

Create a systemized checklist for your clients to follow. This will allow them to clearly see how your program works and how you will guide them through the process. Be sure to ask your clients the right questions up front that will help guide you through the coaching/consulting process. Having a system allows you to put everything in place so that you don't have to reinvent the wheel with each new client you take on. Systems also help to effectively monetize your consulting business because you can take on more clients and get better results.

Pricing Your Consulting Services

One thing that you must learn from this book (if nothing else!) is to always value your expertise and charge what you are worth! This allows you to build more value upfront for your services. Your consulting programs can be offered on a variety of different levels, price points, and time lines. When putting together your consulting services you'll want to work backwards so that you can create a highly paid, consistent income plan. Start by thinking about a realistic income you want to make this year from your consulting services alone. What would that amount be? Once you are clear on how much money you want to make, break that down into how many clients you need to work with to achieve your income goal. When you know this, you have an endpoint and goal in mind.

For example, let's say you have different levels of programs, but your average-priced program is $3,000. To make $100,000 a year at this fee level, you would need to take on 34 clients, or you can increase your coaching programs and the value you offer to $10,000. You would then only need to take on 10 clients to achieve your six-figure goal.

Always keep your end goal (annual income) in mind when pricing your consulting programs. Your main goal should be to keep improving your service programs and value so that you can keep increasing your fees. Your goal is not necessarily to have more clients; your goal should be to have more high-level clients who pay you top dollar for your expertise. This way, you work less and make more. You also get a greater return for those clients who are fortunate enough to work with you.

The more personalized your programs are, the higher your price point should be. Remember, the biggest value you can offer is your time. The number-one thing clients will pay top dollar for is your time. However, time is also the most limiting; you only have so many hours in a day. Therefore, your top-dollar program is the one that offers the most one-on-one personalized time with you, especially if you are meeting with clients face to face. This is the most time-consuming, and therefore should be the most costly investment for your clients.

If you prefer to offer your consulting services by phone, you save a great deal on travel time. Some consultants even work from their home office by phone in their bathrobe (my preferred way of working). I often tease my clients that if they want to set up a Skype call with the video on, I'm going to have to charge them more because I actually have to get dressed and put on makeup. They laugh, but part of me is serious about this because it all takes time.

Add Personalized VIP Days to Your Consulting Services

One of the best ways to work with clients on high-end programs is to set up personalized VIP days. These can be done live in person, but they are more time-saving when done via telephone, Skype, or Google Hangout. Consider setting up high-end consulting programs working a half day or full day with your clients by phone. There is little set-up time needed to prepare for VIP days; all you'll need to do is a pre-consulting questionnaire and/or call to discover your clients' needs. Next, develop a program through which you can guide and consult them. Plan on taking a number of breaks during the call to allow your client to work on an assignment and clear her head. Personalized VIP days can give your clients great value by working to achieve fast results for them. Some experts charge from $1,500 to $5,000 or more for a half or full VIP day by phone, whereas personalized face-to-face consulting programs can run from $3,500 to $25,000 or more per day depending on the consultant's level of expertise, the ROI he offers, and his specific target market.

My client Phil, a sales consultant, started out offering high-end consulting programs, and the first month we launched he was asking $20,000 for his services. I was amazed that he gained a client at that level so quickly. This rarely happens when you first launch a consulting program, but Phil was clear on the number of clients he wanted to work with, his level of his experience, and what his income goal was. He wanted only high-end clients and not a lot of them; for those clients, he was willing to give more of his personal time.

Offering E-mail Access Is Also Personalized Time

Consider offering personalized e-mail access as part of your overall program. For example, I offer my clients unlimited e-mail access with a quick response within 48 hours or less. The value of your clients having a lifeline to you like this is huge! You may end up getting a lot of e-mails; I certainly do. But when you develop a system of training your clients to communicate effectively with you and work through your step-by-step program, you can get a lot of work done in a short amount of time.

Keep in mind that if you're going to offer unlimited e-mail access, you can't wait for days to respond to your clients, unless you have communicated to them that you are off of e-mail for a certain amount of time due to travel, holidays, and so on. Otherwise you need to follow up quickly. If you offer this service you should be keeping up with your e-mail every day; at minimum, every other day. E-mail allows you to keep the communication flowing with your clients. It allows you to get information out quickly, share files, move through a systemized program, and so on.

If you don't want to be glued to your e-mail account, allow your clients a select number of e-mails per month instead. Remember that the highly paid expert works within his freedom lifestyle, the way he best prefers to work for himself and his clients.

Along with personalized time via phone or in person and e-mail access, you can also add online training materials as a bonus. Throw product downloads into your program as well. This way, your client can continue to learn from your expert advice without utilizing your personal time. Downloadable products offer great value to your clients and cost you nothing in return.

Group-Level Consulting

Another way to offer your consulting is through group calls. When you do group calls, you can take on more clients, but the perceived value is less than for one-on-one consulting time. One way to increase the value you offer for group calls is to add a personalized Q&A forum in which you answer questions live on the call. You can either open up your phone line for smaller groups or have your clients send in their questions ahead of time via e-mail. Make this a first-come basis, such that clients must be on the call live to receive your personalized response. Group calls can also be offered in your coaching programs at all levels as well. This adds more value to your overall packaged service programs.

Manifest Your Highly Paid Expert Lifestyle

Consulting is a wonderful career that allows you to give from your wisdom and your heart. It allows you to share your expert skills with others and guide your clients to achieve goals, overcome obstacles, inspire hope and encouragement, empower change, make more money, and much more.

There are many ways to set up your consulting programs. There is no one specific way that works for every expert. Set up your own unique programs that fit into your highly paid expert lifestyle, and always keep your annual income goal in mind.

Seek out action-takers, clients who are ready to go, people who want your support to move. Take on high-level clients who understand your value and are eager to invest in your services.

You will manifest the exact type of clients and income you want to achieve when you are clear with your goals, value, and overall business vision.

CHAPTER 15

OFFER SOLUTIONS TO PROBLEMS

As an expert, you will be most remembered by the problems you solve for your clients with your expertise. You deal with problems that might otherwise seem huge, overwhelming, or excessively complex to others. Don't take your knowledge and expertise for granted. Your way of looking at things, your way of thinking, is unique, and it is based upon your own experiences, failures, and successes. That's what your clients pay for. You offer them a shortcut to problem-solving. You help by moving them away from obstacles that are stunting their growth and you guide them in the right direction for expansion.

When you discover how to best solve your clients' problems, you begin to develop more value as an expert. Find a way to offer your expert value in an innovative way—this is called *value innovation*. It requires a unique way of looking at the obstacles and challenges your clients face. Try to discover your own unique way of offering strategic logic along with good common sense and personal experiences to help solve problems for others.

Experts Help to Make Problems Go Away

Good problem-solving skills are fundamentally important if you're going to be successful as an expert. Problems are something we all want to get rid of; they are costly, time-consuming, and stressful. Problems force us to think about an uncertain future, and some seem to never go away.

That's why, when faced with problems, your clients want to eliminate them as quickly as possible. They want to find the easiest and most obvious solution, and that solution should be to work with you!

To be an effective problem-solver, you need to be systematic and logical at the same time. When you solve problems you help others make more effective decisions that can improve their personal or professional lives. And as you increase your problem-solving skills, you also increase your own confidence and value as an expert.

Five Steps to Improving Your Problem-Solving Skills

◆ **Step 1: Define each problem in detail before trying to solve it.** Take time to understand the problem, understand the criteria for a good decision, and generate some good options.

◆ **Step 2: Offer one or two firmly suggested solutions.** Offering too many suggestions will only confuse your client and allow him to become indecisive.

◆ **Step 3: Prioritize your client's action steps to help avoid him or her feeling overwhelmed.** If your client agrees to take action, ask him to relax and focus on moving forward.

◆ **Step 4: Implement a step-by-step plan of action.** When you approach problems systematically, you cover the essentials each time—and your decisions are well-thought-out, well-planned, and well-executed.

◆ **Step 5: Look for more ways to improve upon the problem-solving idea to avoid future problems.** Continue to perfect your problem-solving skills and use them for continuous improvement initiatives to serve your clients' needs.

Proactive Problem-Solving Sets Your Clients Up for Success

Some problems are obvious; others are not so easily identified. Proactive problem-solving can help your clients avoid future emergencies. Set your clients up for success by identifying problems that could arise in the future based upon other experiences you've had working with clients or from your own personal experiences. By educating your clients in advance, you will help them to remain calm and in control when issues or challenges arise.

Be sure that you are watching changes in your clients' needs and market dynamics. Monitor trends that are relevant to your expertise. Experts are always on top of their game by becoming educated way ahead of industry standards.

After identifying a potential problem, you need information:

◆ What factors contribute to the problem?

◆ Who is involved with it?

◆ What solutions have been tried before?

◆ What do others think about the problem?

If you move forward to find a solution for your client too quickly, you risk relying on imperfect information that's based on assumptions and limited perspectives, so make sure you research the problem thoroughly.

Once you understand the problem, define it clearly and completely. Next, establish specific boundaries for solving it. This keeps the scope from growing too large and allows you to step back and open your mind to a much sharper and more comprehensive definition to the problem. With a clear problem definition, start generating ideas for a solution. The key here is to be flexible in the way you approach a problem. You want to be able to see it from as many expert perspectives as possible. Looking for patterns or common elements in different parts of the problem can sometimes help.

When solving problems for my clients, I often use traditional brainstorming; this allows my client and me to work as a team. Working as a team also helps to get my clients to "buy in to" my suggestions, because they are ideas that came directly from the brainstorming and reverse-brainstorming process. When you take the time to generate a range of creative solutions to the problem as a team, you'll significantly increase the likelihood that you'll find the best possible solution, and not just a one-sided approach.

After developing ideas, decide what elements are needed for a realistic and practical solution, and think about the criteria and steps required between potential solutions. For example, I help my clients create a quick-cash action plan that offers the solution of generating income fast. To do this I need to first discover the problems my clients may have related to their marketing that blocks opportunities to get more prospects and make more sales. Once I've discovered the problem or marketing obstacles that are blocking their success, I make suggestions and offer solutions that will allow money to flow to them faster and easier.

You might think that choosing a solution is the end of a problem-solving process. In fact, it's simply the start of the next phase in problem-solving: implementation. This involves lots of planning and preparation. It's important to let your client know how to prepare as you begin to roll out your proposed solution. For smaller projects, action plans can be put into place, but for larger projects you'll need to be able to help with change management as well.

As part of the planning process, you must convince your client that your expert solution is the best one. You'll likely meet with resistance, so before you try to "sell" your idea, make sure you've considered all the consequences. As you begin communicating your plan, listen to what your client has to say and make adjustments as necessary. The better the overall solution meets your client's needs, the greater its positive impact will be!

Finally, once you've convinced your client that your proposed solution is worth running with, you can move on to the implementation/action stage. This is the exciting and rewarding part of problem-solving, which makes the whole process worthwhile for an expert. The more value you bring to your client, the more she will pay for your advice.

CHAPTER 16

GROW YOUR EXPERT COMMUNITY

GROWING YOUR EXPERT COMMUNITY BOTH ONLINE and offline is extremely important for building a highly paid expert business. First you must develop a strategy that builds a following. Your following includes Facebook fans, Twitter followers, YouTube subscribers, and e-mail subscribers. In most cases, strategy to build a community is an afterthought, yet it's your Golden Database that will allow your expert business to thrive. Followers in your own community equate to income!

Your expert community will only grow when you begin to think outside of the box. You must be creative and up to date with your marketing. You must not only be creative, but you must also think about building a community that belongs to only you; nobody else has access to your list. With this type of community, you are able to simply push a button to reach them. Having your own expert community is powerful and critically important to becoming a highly paid expert.

Turn Seekers Into Community Followers

Online domination and search engine optimization is all about the process of delivering **seekers** to your Website. Yet there are different types of followers that will join your community; it's important to understand who they are and why they are following you. Some are simply seeking information. They may have come across a post, video, or Web link you posted. The seeker may just be checking you out at first, but once he opts into your database, he becomes part of *your* expert community. It is as if he were raising his hand to say, "I respect your expertise and I want you to stay in touch with me." But the thing about seekers is that they may not stay with you for very long; once they get their fill of information or find what they need, they may leave you. They are a sponge for information. That's why it's important to engage the seeker early on to keep him onboard in your community.

The **social sharer** shares and promotes your expertise to her following. Social media followers can help you increase the power of your online posts by cross-promoting on other social media platforms. As long as they continue to follow you, they are shameless fans of your work and gain pleasure from posting and re-posting your advice. Keep them engaged by recognizing them and thanking them for their efforts.

The **born follower** will quickly like your page and follow you wherever you guide him. He likes to join and become engaged with experts. Some may simply follow you just because you already have a big following. Once they are inspired by your brand and expertise, you can easily turn this type of follower into a warm prospect and even a buyer early on because they simply need engagement to take action.

Gain a Targeted Online Community

To gain a targeted following and become known online, you must create valuable expert content and encourage sharing of your information. The content you create must offer real value to your target market. This sounds pretty simple, but quality often gets left behind in favor of quantity. Your content must intend to solve a pain or problem that your target audience is facing, and it must also showcase you as the expert in this area. Great content sent once per week via e-mail will keep your new followers engaged. This is what they call *education-based marketing*. There are two types of content. One should be lead-generating content such as articles, e-books, free guidebooks, and interviews that provide a call to action for your followers to join you. The second type should be educational content that is intended to share helpful, quality information that will showcase your expertise, such as training videos, Webinars, teleseminars, and Google Hangouts.

Become Social With Your Followers

Begin listening and connecting with your followers so that they can learn more about you or your business right away. If you don't engage them, they won't be encouraged to stay in your community. Sites like Facebook, Google+, and LinkedIn allow you to join your targeted communities, connect with them, and share information they find valuable.

To gain an expert following, you'll need to give people a reason to follow you. Never underestimate the importance of sharing bits of personal information about yourself. Some of the best connections I've ever made were as a direct result of something personal I've posted online. Even a kind word or a comment post could gain you a following to your community. Be sure to spend time only on social media sites that will ensure a return in followers to your community. Your results will be directly proportional to how many people join your e-mail list.

The best way to grow your email list is to do it slowly and continuously so that the people on your list are really engaged. You want high-quality followers to join and stay in your community. This way, you will gain the best results from your e-mail marketing efforts.

One way to build high-quality followers is to keep sending out relevant educational content on a consistent basis. It's not about sending out an e-mail newsletter once in a while. You must be consistent and strategic. Another way to keep your community active is to really touch the hearts and minds of your followers by engaging them in your personal life.

Important! To grow your opt-in list you *must* have a signup form on the home page of your Website; this is a *must*! Free offers create fast lead generation. Offer a free gift for signing up such as an e-book or e-guide. An e-book is usually about 40 to 100 pages, and a simple e-guide is only about 10 to 20 pages. Both work well as a free offer to convert followers into your community. Keep in mind it's not about the number of pages you provide; it's about making a good offer to get followers to take action.

The information you provide in your free offer will inform prospects of your expertise and give them some quick tips. Normally I suggest sharing seven to 10 tips that solve a problem related to your expertise. Your free offer can also be easily created by using a series of articles. Or if you have already written a book, simply break it down into a short booklet or offer a free chapter. It's important that your free offer also has a call to action at the bottom so that you can move the reader to the next opportunity of working with you. For example, your call to action at the end of a free book chapter would be to ask your reader to buy your book.

Once your free offer is in place, you'll also need to set up an auto-responder program and an e-mail management system such as MailChimp.com, AWeber.com, ConstantContact.com, or Infusion Soft to automate your list. Your free offer can be used on a landing page, your main corporate Website, or both.

Your first auto-responder is a thank-you e-mail, thanking your followers for opting in. This same e-mail can then direct your new followers to more information and/or give another call to action. Additional auto-responder messages will keep prospects in the loop by offering them access to your newsletter and ongoing marketing messages.

It's important to test your auto-responder system and every e-mail before sending them out to make sure they look professional.

Five Ways to Grab More Followers

1. Put a link to your signup form on every page of your Website. Also add a link on the footer of your page or side navigation.

2. Place a link to your e-mail signup form in your e-mail signature along with your free gift offer.

3. Offer a free giveaway to lucky subscribers.

4. Place a link at the bottom of your articles that leads to your free online offer and opt-in form.

5. Place a link on social media sites that leads to your free offer and opt-in form.

Do It the Right Way

Avoid doing it the wrong way. Purchasing or renting (or, worse yet, stealing) a list is the worst way to build a following. It's not illegal to purchase a list, but it's not something most e-mail management companies will allow. Sending bulk e-mail to a purchased list is the definition of spam, and no one likes a spammer. Poorly managed e-mail practices can get your e-mails blocked and/or cause more followers from your community to drop off.

Even if you already have an e-mail list of customers with whom you've been doing business for years, you should still ask them if they want to opt in to your newsletter or free offer. You should always ask for permission; it's more effective, and best of all, it's polite. An easy way to do this is to send a re-introduction e-mail. Make it a more personalized message. Write it as if you were writing to a friend. Then include the link to your sign-up form and make it easy for them to join your community.

As you build your expertise online, your online community will continue to grow. It takes time to do it the right way, but when you do, you'll keep your followers longer. Remember that followers on social media are not followers in your community; you must get them to opt in to grow your expert community.

CHAPTER 17

BUILD A HIGHLY PAID SPEAKING PLATFORM

CAN YOU IMAGE HAVING A CAREER IN WHICH YOU get paid well to share your wisdom, inspiration, and advice, all while you travel the world on someone else's dime? Sounds like a good gig, huh? That's the life I lived as a professional speaker for nearly 20 years. I've presented in 28 countries and experienced more adventure and culture than I could have ever imagined.

There is a big difference between a paid professional speaker who speaks to receive a fee and an expert who educates to sell. They are two completely different approaches to the speaking business. Having been paid well to speak and travel for years, I would never have imagined that speaking for free and traveling at my own expense would ever be a viable option again, but it turned out to be the best move I could have made. Allow me to explain in more detail.

Getting Paid to Speak

In order to succeed as a paid professional speaker, the speaker's message must be connected to the needs and aspirations of the audience. The professional must also be skilled as a speaker to get paid well for presenting. The main goals of a paid professional speaker are to train and/or motivate without selling. The speaker must be good enough to get invited back to present again at a future event and/or get referrals for additional paid speaking engagements. Paid professional speakers must count on getting enough bookings based upon their fee to make a good income.

Paid professional speakers normally get paid 50 percent of their speaking fee once they have secured the booking. The other 50 percent of the fee plus travel expenses are paid upon the speaker's arrival at the event; therefore, they take on little or no risk of their own. A professional speaker's responsibility is to show up and deliver the best motivational and/or educational speech he can. Sounds easy, but actually it's not. Most professional speakers take years to perfect their art before they get their first paid booking. When professional speakers begin their career, they must be willing to work for free and travel at their own expense just to get known. And if they don't have the opportunity to sell when they speak for free, it is a costly way to grow a business. In addition, staying fresh and relevant is critical for professional speakers to remain successful. They must always be working toward improving their craft of speaking.

As an expert, you may not have years to work on perfecting your speaking skills to the point that you get paid to speak. Paid professional speaking is also a hard way to make big money unless you become well known for your expertise. Only a handful of professional speakers make six figures or more annually from their fees alone. The average professional speaker typically makes about $45,000 a year. Professional speakers do not work a standard 40-hour week; instead they work by engagement. They must stay booked to make a decent living, and that takes constant marketing efforts. The average number of speaking engagements for professionals is typically between 20 and 30 per year.

Paid professionals, or what is often referred to as motivational speakers, are also experts who speak. The majority typically get paid between $1,500 and $5,500 per speech. The fee depends on the experience of the speaker, who the speaker is, and what the topic is. Many paid professional speakers belong to the National Speakers Association (NSASpeaker.org). The top 10 percent of professionals within this association who have honed their craft can earn up to $175,000 per year. That's a small percentage of professionals who make that type of income from paid professional speaking alone.

Fame and recognition often dictate the demand for professionals. Celebrity speakers can get paid very well due to the draw of their name alone. Others need to subsidize their income by selling their books or home study courses at the back of the room at their speaking engagement. But the problem with being a paid professional is that you are rarely invited to sell, because you are getting paid to speak.

The majority of professional speakers are self-employed and pay their salaries from their profits. Some motivational speakers have bachelor's or master's degrees in business, theology, finance, or communications (whichever field they are in), but experience and expertise are foremost, not education. For example, I had no college degree, but I had been a highly successful entrepreneur since the young age of 19, so I used this as my uniqueness and my platform. My expertise came from my own life experiences, as well as building and selling companies in diverse industries. My continued education came from hiring experts at every level, from whom I learned advanced business and marketing skills.

Paid professional speakers must also have the ability to lead, inspire, and relate to their audiences. Other essential requirements are charisma, stamina, wit, and writing and storytelling skills. Paid professional speakers provide uplifting messages, the purpose of which can be anything from personal motivation to growing a business. Their goal would be to get a standing ovation vs. having people run to the back of the room to buy from them.

My Professional Speaking Career

After many years of training and experience as a paid professional speaker, I became one of the top three percent of professional women speakers in the world when I was honored with my CSP, or Certified Speaking Professional designation, by the National Speakers Association. My speaking fee at the time was $8,500 for a keynote presentation, which was earning me a quarter of a million dollars a year from speaking alone. My target market had shifted into three main industries: retail, real estate, and mortgage. All the income streams I had at the time were flowing well: speaking, my own events, and my real estate investments. The speaking business had served me well and life was good. But things were soon about to change.

The real estate bubble in the U.S. housing marketing collapsed, causing many industries to shift dramatically. The economy began to plummet, and so did my speaking business. Because I was speaking a lot in the real estate and mortgage industry, my speaking engagements dropped dramatically. It was also harder to fill seats for my live events because people had less money to invest. My real estate investments also took a dive. The U.S. economy was in serious trouble, and almost everyone was feeling the financial pressure, including me. Overall, meetings in the United States were drastically cut and opportunities for most paid professional speakers fell way off. It was not looking good for the professional speaking business.

Luckily, I have one business skill that I can always count on, and that is to see through obstacles and figure out a creative way to reinvent. It was time for change and reinvention if I was going to survive in the paid speaking business. Because I had years of experience and expertise in the speaking business already, I knew I could get hired more often if I could find more opportunities. But just where were those opportunities? Then I thought, *There's a big world out there that needs to hear my message, and I just need a focus outside of the United States to gain more opportunity.* One thing I strongly believe is that everything happens for a reason. We may not know the reason at the time, but if we pay attention, it will usually show up.

> *When you start paying closer attention to opportunities, they will appear all around you.*

New opportunities began to appear before me; I actually found it fairly easy to get speaking opportunities outside of the United States due to the level of expertise and skills I had developed from my entrepreneurial background. Within just three months of shifting my marketing efforts, 85 percent of my speaking business was overseas.

During my international travels, I also found a new interest and started attending multi-speaker events where I saw experts educating to *sell*. Ding ding! Another opportunity was placed in front of me that I wouldn't have seen before the well dried up. Learning how to sell from the stage opened new and exciting ways for me to eventually make even more money as an expert who speaks. Yet this was a

360-degree turnabout from my paid professional speaking business.

When I started my speaking career back in 1995, I had to do a number of speaking engagements for free or for next to nothing. And now I was right back where I had started (or so I thought). This was a completely different way of doing business than the way I had known, and that caused a challenging mental shift for me. I was going from being one of the top paid professional speakers in the world to now having an opportunity to speak for "free" in return for possibly selling. I was also paying all my own travel expenses and taking all the risk.

Speaking to Sell

Experts who speak strictly for the opportunity to sell must be able to connect with the audience enough that people will trust and buy from them. They need to be good speakers, but they don't have to be great speakers, as long as they know how to educate the audience and sell their services and products effectively from the stage. If not, they don't get paid! When there is an opportunity to sell from the stage, the expert who educates to sell must have a message that directly showcases the value and benefits of what they have to offer in such a way that the audience buys from them on the spot. They have one main goal in mind for their presentation, and that is to sell! Experts who educate to sell also have the opportunity to walk away with an endless amount of income based upon their sales.

Both types of speaking require a different set of expert skills, and both are excellent ways to showcase your expertise. As an expert, it's important to not only learn how to present well, but also learn how to sell effectively from the stage. Both of these skills will serve you well.

At first I was having a hard time learning how to close sales from the stage. Often I would walk away without a paycheck and piles of expenses. Sometimes the risk was huge, when I traveled halfway around the world on my own dime and had no sales to show for it. Zero, zip, nada! (Important note: Practice selling in your own area first before flying halfway around the world trying to figure it out like I did.)

Sometimes I would make a few sales, but certainly not as much as my paid speaking fees; most of the time I would bomb and walk away with little or no sales at all to show for my efforts. This was frustrating and costly. I was getting tired of losing money going it alone, but I was still determined to keep trying to learn the ropes and the skill of selling from the stage. I watched other experts sell from the stage and tried to figure it out. Many of them were not even good speakers, but they sure could sell! I was determined to learn this skill and learn it well. And like most things, hiring an expert who was already skillful at this was the way to go. There are a number of experts who can teach you how to speak to sell at their workshops, but most of us need some personalized guidance to learn this skill. This is because every speaker and every sales opportunity is going to be different.

After too many failed attempts, I decided to find an expert to work with whom I saw knock it out of the park with her sales. She told me she learned the skill by paying another expert $25,000 to teach him the art of selling from the stage. So I made the same offer to this expert. She helped me put together my presentation slide by slide, and walked me through the steps on exactly what to say and how to close the sale. I quickly put these lessons to work, and my investment paid off right away. That's when I took my paid professional speaking business to a lucrative educate-to-sell model.

*Life often hands us obstacles so that we are forced
to reinvent a new way of doing things.*

Highly Paid Experts Know the Secrets of Selling From the Stage

Selling from the stage is not magic; there is a definite science and a system that can be taught to just about anyone. This is an exciting opportunity for experts. Here's the first big secret: To sell effectively from the stage you must work backwards from your presentation. What does that mean? Your offer and your closing slides are the most important part of the presentation, because your main goal is to sell. Therefore, you must put together your sales offer first, and then develop a presentation that works around your close.

You must give enough information to clearly showcase that you are the go-to expert on the subject, and each of your talking points should solve a problem and/or offer some type of solution. Also keep in mind that you don't want to be a trainer teaching your audience exactly how to do something. When you do this, you give away too much, and that can make your audience believe they can do it on their own without your help (even though they most likely can't do it on their own).

Give your audience just enough information that they understand that *you* are the solution to their problem, and that they need *your* expertise to make positive changes. They will buy when you have shown them you have the answers they are seeking. It's like showing the audience a blueprint to a house, but not giving them the tools to build it on their own. To build it (whatever it may be), they need *your* tools: knowledge, guidance, support, and secrets to success.

The next secret to selling from the stage is to have a PowerPoint presentation that visually showcases your offer. Your presentation must be designed effectively to trigger (with integrity) people to take action immediately. There is a very specific sequence of steps required in your presentation to make the perfect pitch (or what I like to call your offer).

I love teaching other experts how to educate to sell their services from the stage because my students gain such fast results. I've taught even the shyest people how to speak and close from the stage. I've even taught this skill to people who said they hated selling, by showing they don't actually have to sell; they simply need to learn how to communicate the offer and invite people to buy. This skill can be life-changing. At my High-Paid Speaker Training events (HighPaidSpeakerTraining.com), I teach other experts exactly how to put together a PowerPoint presentation that will dramatically and instantly increase their sales. It's a personalized, hands-on approach. Students leave the event after a couple of days with not only the skills of selling, but also with a locked and loaded presentation ready to close more sales. Most students easily increase their sales by two or three times the next time they speak.

Experts Need to Become Good Salespeople

Just as professional paid speaking is an art, so is learning how to educate to sell. Most paid professional speakers are not good at selling because they feel uncomfortable with it. If you aren't comfortable selling, or don't think you are good at it, get over it and learn how! Okay, I will admit that selling from the stage made me uncomfortable at first too. But it's just like anything else that you attempt for the first time: you may need to feel uncomfortable at first, and even fall down a few times, before you can run.

As an expert, you must know how to ask for the sale. It doesn't matter if you plan to speak on a stage to sell, or sell from a teleseminar, it's still selling. The key to selling from the stage is preparation. When you are informed and prepared with the right phrases and the right practices, it becomes easier and more comfortable. Vocal rehearsal and practice is one of the most effective ways to remove discomfort from a sales approach.

Your audience will seldom think you are being pushy when you ask them to make a buying decision, unless you use manipulative sales tactics, aggressive closing lines, or the wrong tone of voice. When done effectively, selling from the stage doesn't have to be pushy at all; it's simply a conversational offer that can support the success of others. When you look at it this way, it takes the "pushy" out of being "sales-y."

The key to setting yourself up well for the close is to ensure that you have effectively identified a potential problem, and you have offered a solution in terms that make sense to your audience. When you've done this well, your audience will be ready to buy. **Important:** Keep in mind that you are *not* selling "items," such as books, CDs or even services. You don't sell *items*; you sell results, solutions, and support!

You may still be thinking, *I don't like to sell, so maybe I'll skip this part and just work on building a paid professional speaking business where people pay me to speak and I won't have to sell.* I respect your position on this; I was there myself, for a long time. But to become a highly paid expert, this is one skill you must be open to, otherwise your income will be limited. The fear or discomfort some people have about selling is expensive; this fear or discomfort can actually rob you of massive leverage that creates massive sales. So, before you dismiss the opportunity or think that selling to an audience could not possibly be for you, read on.

There is too much opportunity here for you to ignore! We all understand that good salespeople have the opportunity to create unlimited income instead of just collecting a flat salary. Commissioned salespeople take on the risk that they can sell for the opportunity to make more money in the long run. Because they take more risk than a salaried person, they also reap more rewards when they sell well. No one wants to be sold to, but we all enjoy buying. Personally I don't like aggressive salespeople at all; they can be a real turn-off! But when selling is done well—i.e., in the service of others—it becomes a win/win.

Selling can actually be fun. To enjoy the selling process, you'll first need to eliminate any personal biases you have about selling. This may be easier said than done. The key is to first identify your own personal beliefs related to selling and asking for the sale. Once you identify the beliefs that could be holding you back, it will be easier to begin to believe differently.

Selling does not have to be aggressive. You obviously have the skills and knowledge as an expert to help others, so what's to sell? Selling from the stage is actually more about educating, informing, and inviting others to work with you so that you can support them in return. Sounds like a win/win to me. Think about it this way: If you don't sell, you are not only doing yourself a disservice, you are doing a huge disservice to all the people you can't help. So by not selling, you actually take away the opportunity to support more people.

Use Visuals to Help Increase Your Sales

Most of us are visual learners: We gain more from a visual presentation than the spoken word. That's why using PowerPoint (or Keynote for Mac) is the best way to enhance your presentation and improve your sales. So let's say you have been invited to speak to showcase your expertise. You have to make some sales, so the stakes are high. You have been fretting over each PowerPoint slide for weeks, because every word of your presentation and every slide must be perfect and in exactly the right order if you are to close the sale. Your mission is to lay down a faultlessly planned and executed sales strategy that persuades the audience to buy. To do this, you must learn how to create a dynamic sales presentation that helps you easily overcome any objective and move your audience to your closing opportunity.

The problem that most experts run into when they try to sell using PowerPoint is they plow through way too much information and mountains of bullet-point slides to get to the point, and then they rush the sale. Rushing the sale will kill your sales opportunities every time. Remember, as an expert who educates to sell, your main goal is to make sales. Everything you share in your presentation must lead or seed to the close. Your audience (or prospects) will value what you have to offer and will be less concerned about the price if your solutions are clearly relevant to their immediate problems. As a speaker, you solve problems the same way a coach or consultant does. Your prospects want to know the value of what the final outcome will be from your solutions as an expert.

The Sky's the Limit

Highly paid experts are world-class salespeople because they do what most people are too scared to do. The good news is that selling your expertise is actually easier than you may think. Imagine selling more than $100,000 in just 90 minutes from the stage, or making more than half a million dollars in one weekend hosting your own event. This is exactly what I did when I shifted my speaking business from paid professional speaking to selling from stage. Once this happened, I was hooked on a new way of using my speaking skills as an expert. Selling from the stage is actually easy when you've been shown, step by step, exactly how to do it. All the secrets and little-known tricks of the trade have helped to make my students very successful. This is a strategy and skill that they can use for a lifetime to create an endless stream of abundance.

Experts all have products and services to sell that add value to people's lives, and people are willing to do whatever it takes to hear what you have to say when you have a solution that will help them. How much would an extra 10, 20, or 100 new customers mean to your business and your income? There is no other sales technique that compares to your ability to move your customers to action by demonstrating the benefits of your offer in real life, and amplifying the result by speaking directly to an audience who shows up to listen to your expertise.

If you limit yourself to only paid professional speaking and/or selling online through social media, or any other methods in which you avoid in-person contact with the person you are selling to, you are missing out on a massive opportunity to dramatically increase your income. And furthermore, your prospects are missing out on the opportunity of being able to see you speak at a live event in supporting their success.

CHAPTER 18

SELL HIGH-END PRODUCTS ONLINE

IN THIS CHAPTER, YOU ARE GOING TO LEARN HOW to make big sales from your expertise, all while working your own hours. You can create an audience of your own right from your home, and best of all, you don't even need to get dressed up. Heck, you can even sell in your morning bathrobe if you wish (shhh...no one will ever know). As a highly paid expert, you want to build a successful business around *your* values, family, and lifestyle, not the other way around. You want a freedom lifestyle in which you can do business your own way.

Many businesses require you to put your business above everything else, but the expert business isn't one of them. Highly paid experts don't play small, focusing on selling a $20 book or a $97 product; they play big by focusing on creating and selling high-end products that can produce as much as six figures—or more—selling directly through teleseminars or Webinars. And best of all, you don't even have to leave the comfort of your own home to do this! Having a large database helps to make this a reality, but if you don't already have a list, you can get started right away by leveraging the power of joint venture partners, social media leads, and free preview calls.

Start With a Free Preview Class

Teleseminars are the easiest, fastest, and least expensive way to get those big-money paydays with very little investment on your part. I always teach my students to start out with teleseminars to develop quick sales and fast product development for this very reason. They can get clients easily this way if they have already learned how to educate to sell.

Webinars are another great way to showcase your expertise. In fact, I love the visual aspect that Webinars have to keep viewers' attention, and closing with PowerPoint can be very effective. But Webinars do require a bit more technical skill to run than teleseminars. Therefore, if you don't already have the skill to create good PowerPoint presentations or you don't know how to set these up, begin by hosting a tele-class by phone first. It's the easiest path. If you can pick up a phone and push a button to record the call, you're good to go.

Teleseminars and Webinars are both great ways to keep prospects on your list by offering them more value. They attract more clients and can also create amazing information products to build passive income streams. Best of all, you don't need a big marketing budget, and you don't need to travel to make either one of these happen. Now with that being said, it doesn't mean you can ignore the power of getting in front of a live audience. In my opinion, nothing beats selling in front of a live audience. But those opportunities are not always going to be in front of you. Plus, selling by phone or Webinar creates an additional stream of speaking income. Some experts have gotten very good at this, but again, it's a different skill set to master from selling from the stage.

Put Together Your Classes and Marketing Plan Well in Advance

If you want to make money online, you need to focus on setting up a marketing system that drives your prospects to become listeners and eventually buyers. Most preview calls are free to attend. If you are setting up a series of calls, you may want to charge a fee, especially if you are offering your attendees recordings of the classes. Fees for these classes can range anywhere from $49 up to hundreds of dollars. Remember that you want to set your entry fee lower if you plan to sell at the end of call or the end of the series.

With a series of classes, you can also develop instant product. This is a fast, easy, and low-cost way to develop your expert products. To develop your series, you'll first need to come up with a catchy title for your overall series, and then write out six to eight punchy topic titles for your classes. Keep in mind that your class titles must be powerful enough to get people to take action to register and also to show up, even if they are free. Next, select the date(s) that you will present your classes. The best days and times of the week for teleseminars and Webinars are typically Tuesday, Wednesday, or Thursday in the early evening hours.

If you are setting up a teleseminar, you can use a free call service, such as FreeConferencePro.com or FreeConferenceCall.com. These services are free to use, and they also offer free recording services. Register with one of these and practice recordings before your first call, and be sure to grab a copy of your recordings right after the call to ensure they don't get erased. These free services will only continue to host your free call line if it remains active. They also won't hold your recordings online for an extended period of time. These free providers offer a good place to begin, but they do limit your options. You can sign up for paid services that charge you a monthly fee. They have options from the basic level at $47 up to guru level at $197 a month, depending on the number of participants and services you want to utilize. Companies such as InstantTeleseminars.com or GoToWebinar.com offer more bells and whistles to your class options for both teleseminars and Webinars. Additional services include such items as online streaming, Q&A options, a "who's on the call" dashboard, multiple-host access, and more.

Get Them to Show Up and Buy

The easy part is getting ready for the call and actually delivering the class. Any expert can do this, but not every expert can turn the call into a sales opportunity. To make this happen, you must have a system in place that fills the call funnel and produces your end result: more sales.

First of all, you need to get prospective buyers on the call with you. What this takes is good copywriting that leads to signups. Even a free call needs good e-mail copy and great follow-up to fill your classes. It's vital that you put all the pieces in place before you launch, or it is unlikely you will make big sales at the end of your call. It doesn't matter how fabulous your talk is; if no one hears or sees it, you won't make sales, and that's why filling your classes is important.

Although filling your classes is extremely important, I'm not telling you to wait until you have a huge database to begin your first class. Even if you only have a few prospects and your best friend and her cat on the call, you can still get started and gain results. You may not make a lot of sales when you start out, but you will be creating product that can generate ongoing sales for additional streams of income. This is one of the easiest and fastest ways to create your first information product, because you can build it while getting paid at the same time. Once you get people on the call, you will need to have a well-crafted presentation that informs and closes sales. This part is critical to making money from teleseminars and Webinars.

Remember the secret I shared with you about putting together your closing offer? The secret is to work backwards from your closing offer. You must *first* develop the offer, *before* putting together your presentation. You'll need to lead your listeners by seeding (or suggesting) the close in advance of actually making your offer.

You may want to consider adding handouts that reminds attendees to show up on time. Providing handouts is optional, but I highly suggest it to not only get your attendees ready for the call, but also to keep them following along every step of the way; it's easy for them to listen in and not get side-tracked. Keep them focused on your presentation by asking them to write things down, as this will keep them more involved and active throughout your program. Don't worry about making your handout lengthy or detailed; one or two pages created in a simple PDF format with some fill-in-the-blank sections is all you need. Remember to also add your complete contact information and your closing offer to the handout. Add a download version of your handout to your thank-you page and your e-mail follow-up, and remind listeners to download the handout before each call.

Offer a Trial Close to Get Your Audience Onboard

Another way to seed before you make the closing offer is to offer a "trial close." This applies to all types of speaking to sell. Trial closes are extremely helpful for getting your audience onboard with you before the offer is presented. For example, before going to the close, ask who may be interested in working with you by saying something like, "I know I've only had a short time to share my tips with you today, so I would like to invite you to have the opportunity to learn more. How many of you can see the advantages of learning much more from my expertise?"

If you are in front of a live audience when you make a trial close, you can raise your hand when asking the question. This will automatically get the audience to raise their hands as well. Pay close attention to those hands in the air—they are your possible prospects! When speaking live, you can instantly see how many people might be interested in buying from you, even before you get to your close.

On a tele-class or Webinar, you don't have the opportunity to actually see the audience, so this creates a different dynamic for the sales process. To sell effectively, you'll need to learn how to trial close a bit differently by saying something like, "Thank you so much for coming on the call today; it's been a pleasure sharing some tips with you that you can put into action right away. But I also understand that many of you will not be able to do this all on your own. That's why I would like to offer my support. I know that most of you would say yes to an opportunity to have me personally take you by the hand and walk you through the process step by step, so let me tell you how I can do this for you."

Both of these trial closes can be used to sell personal coaching or even a home-study course (which takes none of your personal time).

You Don't Have to Work Hard to Sell

Again, your closing offer should not feel "pushy" or "sales-y"; if it does, it won't work. Your offer must be a simple, no-brainer offer that perfectly resonates with your ideal target market. Your offer should be so good that listeners can't wait to get out their credit cards to buy before the end of the call. To do this, your offer must be so compelling that it inspires your listeners to buy on the spot. Your offer must also be something that you personally believe in 110 percent. If you don't have a persuasive presentation, you won't make big sales. If you hear prospects telling you that they enjoyed your talk but don't buy, you will continue to miss the mark and lose out on sales.

There are a number of reasons why you might be missing out on sales: your presentation teaches more than it sells, your presentation doesn't directly relate to what you are selling, you have not built up enough value for your offer, you are rushing the close, and/or you aren't comfortable selling. Even by phone, your prospect can feel if you are doubtful and hesitant when you make an offer. On the other hand, prospects can also feel your confidence and enthusiasm. Trust your expertise and what you have to offer, and simply be your real, authentic self. Be clear and on point as you move smoothly and seamlessly from presentation mode to sales mode.

You don't have to work hard selling one prospect at a time, because you can close a lot of people in a tele-class or Webinar at the same time. You also don't need to have a PhD or be an entertainer to host amazing classes that sell by phone or online. When developing your close, consider three reasons why listeners should buy from you: Why you, why the product, and why now?

Selling by phone or online also allows you the freedom to take notes, play with your dog, stand on your head, or whatever works best to make you feel more comfortable. The best part is that listeners can't see you, so you can be sweating it out, but as long as you hold it together and stay on point, no one can tell if you are nervous unless your voice is shaking. You need to feel confident enough that others will invest heavily in what you have to offer, and remain motivated throughout your presentation to get them to take action.

7 Secrets to Increase Your Sales in Every Class

◆ **Secret #1:** Get joint venture affiliates to promote your classes for you. This will increase the numbers on your call and will set you up for success from a referral source.

◆ **Secret #2:** Create a marketing formula with compelling copy that gets prospects to register and show up for the live call.

◆ **Secret #3:** Create hunger and desire in your listeners, even before the call, so they understand how much they need what you're offering and will be ready to take action.

◆ **Secret #4:** Know exactly what motivates your target market as you present your offer.

◆ **Secret #5:** Develop a smooth transition from your presentation to your closing offer. If you flip the switch to sales mode right away, you'll lose your audience and sales.

◆ **Secret #6:** Put together high-value, high-priced packages to increase your bottom line.

◆ **Secret #7:** Develop high-ticket upsell offers. These can be virtual VIP days, one-on-one days, or intimate small-group coaching sessions. Upselling to high-end programs is one of the best and most rewarding income streams available to you as an expert.

CHAPTER 19

GENERATE CASH FLOW FAST WITH VIP DAYS

ALL EDUCATE-TO-SELL PROGRAMS TAKE SKILL AND time to set up, so you may also need a program that can generate quick cash without much skill or effort needed in advance. The answer to this is to offer VIP days. You can begin right away to develop big paydays (even without a list). VIP days don't require a lot of lead time or marketing systems, and they automatically increase your value. Your clients will pay more for personal intensives, and they'll also pay more for speed—clients get better results when they take action quickly. VIP days actually require less time and less work, and most of the time you won't even need to travel, because they can be conducted virtually (by phone or Web), as well as live and in person (near your home). You also don't need to set up a system or a sales page to get started, so you can have your first VIP client in as little as one week. VIP days are great because they are a simple, quick, fast-cash, money-making way to share your expertise.

Develop a Topic and Structure to Support Your Clients

Develop a specific topic and create structure around coaching your clients one on one. Think about what problems you can quickly solve for your clients. Teach them how to overcome a specific problem and *offer them on-the-spot solutions*. This can be done by offering your expert advice and also by brainstorming with your client. When you brainstorm with clients, it helps them to quickly see solutions to their problems. It also reveals other problems that you can help your client solve, opening up multiple opportunities for additional VIP days on different topics.

Set the Pricing for Your VIP Days

Your first level price point could be anywhere from $997 to $9,997 for virtual VIP days and higher for on-site programs. Face-to-face VIP days can range anywhere from $4,997 to $25,000 per day and more for highly paid experts. Normally these are full-day programs done at your location. If the client requests that you to be at his location, your fees will be higher, and your clients will pay all travel-related expenses.

Now you may be thinking, *My clients won't pay that,* or *I have no list to get started.* No worries! All you need to do to set up your VIP days is draw up a breakdown of what your program will offer. Build value around offering more of your personal time. For example, you can include a pre-program questionnaire and a preview call to help your client get ready for her VIP day. Your program may also include a 30- to 60-day e-mail follow-up before and/ or after your VIP day, in order to clarify key points. This guarantees success for both the client and the expert.

When you have an expert program that offers solutions, people will begin paying for your time right away. When you can take someone farther and faster to see immediate results, he will pay even more for your valuable time.

Offering Virtual VIP Intensive Days

Virtual VIP intensive breakthrough days are one of my favorite ways to offer personalized mentoring with my clients. It not only saves me time when it comes to travel, but it saves my clients time and money as well. It's also one of the best ways to gain immediate results. Virtual VIP intensive days are personalized one-on-one business coaching days done via telephone or Skype, focusing on uncovering an action plan for your client that will give her fast turnaround results. For example, my programs focus on helping clients set up their coaching or consulting programs, developing a product, planning an event, setting up a marketing plan, growing their business, and so on. Virtual days allow clients to achieve immediate on-the-spot results through personal guidance and direction.

Virtual days usually run for about four hours. You can set these up by breaking down time slots and assignments so your client doesn't get overwhelmed. Begin by working closely with your client for about 60 minutes, and then take a 30-minute break. Between calls, allow your client the time to gain clarity and/or to complete an assignment. Then get back on the call again for your next session, and so on.

Selling Your VIP Days

You can quickly boost your income with just one powerful and personalized VIP coaching day. VIP days offer you more focus, more momentum, more clients, and more fun. Best of all, you don't need a full-blown sales page to sell your VIP days; that's the beauty of them.

Simply write a few well-crafted e-mails that you can send out over a one-week period that will allow you to gather warm leads. From your e-mails, you can develop and schedule one-on-one conversations to produce buyers. Your message must take the guesswork out of working with you. Let your prospects understand that you will help them to stop spinning their wheels and jumping from idea to idea. Show them how you will keep them from wasting their time and money on strategies that simply don't work.

Your program must offer a clear direction that helps clients gain results from high-payoff activities, such as a focused direction and an implementation plan that will consistently create the fast results they desire. Consider the hundreds of hours your clients will no longer waste trying to learn on their own what you already know.

VIP days are the solution to help your clients cut their learning curve. Be sure to showcase this in all of your e-mail marketing efforts. Saving your prospects time has huge value; they could spend the next two to five years spinning their wheels, trying to figure it out on their own, or you could offer them the solution with quick VIP coaching programs that get them on the fast track to success.

VIP days can also be packaged with your other high-end programs. For example, consider adding a personalized VIP day to your highest-price coaching or consulting program and/or adding it to an existing mastermind program. There are countless ways to add VIP days into your existing programs.

CHAPTER 20

SELL YOUR EXPERTISE AT MULTI-SPEAKER EVENTS

EXPERTS WHO EDUCATE TO SELL ARE ALSO CALLED "platform speakers." They often present at events hosted by someone else. This only works if you sell well from the stage! If not, you won't be invited back to these stages. At these events, you take on less risk, because you only need to pay your own expenses to show up and sell. But before you agree to speak at one of these events, you must be very well prepared!

The host foots the bill for the entire event, and no matter what deal the host may make with his speakers to help fill seats, most speakers don't do a good job of helping them out. The host still holds the responsibility for putting the majority of the butts in the seats—and not just any butts; the right butts! You may have less risk speaking at someone else's event, but you also don't keep all of your sales. Typically you will pay the host 50 percent of your sales income for the opportunity to speak at his event. You also pay your own travel expenses to get to the event in the hopes that the host did a good job of filling the seats with prospective buyers.

Get Ready for the Competition

Speaking on other people's stages to sell your expertise can be a competitive model. This is especially true when you present at what is called a "multi-speaker pitch fest." This is when numerous speakers share the same stage, all trying to get dollars out of the audience. Usually it's a friendly competition, but it's still heavy competition. You have to be really good at selling from the stage to survive these types of events. Typically these events have 12 to 15 speakers throughout a three-day period, and all of the speakers are competing for the same dollars in the room. Because there is only so much money in the room, not all speakers will get their share. But if you do sell well at these multi-speaker events, you can expect to sell anywhere from 15 to 20 percent of the audience. You can figure out what that number comes to by first calculating the number of buying units in the room. What I mean by "buying units" is the possible number of buyers in the room. That doesn't include the entire audience, because some audience members come in pairs. A married couple, for example, would just be one buying unit.

Let's do the math here so you can see the possibilities.

Take an audience size of 200 attendees. Out of this, let's say your prospects where high and you had 150 possible buying units in the audience. Typically the price point offered by most experts at these multi-speaker events run anywhere from $997 to $4,997. So, if you sold 15 percent of the buying units, you would make about 22 sales. And if your offer was on the low end of $997, your total sales would be $21,934. After you pay 50 percent of the sales to your host, you walk away with $10,967, less your expenses. If your price point was $1,997 with the same number of sales, your total sales would be $43,934, and your 50-percent take would be $21,967, less the same amount of expenses. Always do these calculations before you ever agree to speak. Of course, your host cannot guarantee the exact number of people who will attend or who will buy, but you can get a fairly good idea of what your sales could be if all goes well.

The majority of event hosts are honest and work hard to put on top-notch successful events for both their audience and their speakers. The best event hosts also work hard at building long-term joint venture partnerships with their speakers and treat them with respect. For the most part, my experience speaking to sell at other hosted events has been good. As for my own experience as an event host, I no longer want to host multi-speaker pitch-fest events. Yes, I've done them in the past and have made a lot of money from them. In fact, I was one of the first women hosts to actually do this on a grand scale back in 2005. But times have changed, and rarely do these heavy pitch-fest events pay off well for the host, the speakers, or the attendees.

Today people want to attend events where they get more in-depth training. At my events, I now do the majority of the training myself and only bring in a few other speakers that compliment what I have to offer. I've worked with dozens of high-level speakers throughout the years. Most of them have been very professional to work with. Most do what they say they are going to do: help you fill some seats, and do a great job speaking and selling on stage. But a few do a poor job at following up and they don't pay the host on time. It's upsetting to me when I need to chase down one of my speakers to follow up with me or, worse yet, pay me on time. Those speakers won't be asked back to speak on my stage, and they won't be referred by me to any other host's stages. They miss out on a huge opportunity for more business by acting unprofessionally.

So what I'm saying here is, always follow up and always pay your host on time. Typically the host will be paid within 30 days from the date of the event. This allows time to process the sales, follow up with clients, handle any possible cancellations, or set up payment plans. Note that all payment plans should also be approved by your host because you are sharing in the sales. You should be working together as a trusted team!

Do Your Homework Before You Agree to Speak

Just as there are unethical speakers out there, there are a select number of unethical hosts. I've been burned by them a few times myself. That's why I'm much more selective with the number of multi-speaker events at which I agree to speak. Do your homework by asking the host the right questions in advance.

Here are some important questions to ask before you agree to speak:

◆ How many events have you hosted in the past?

◆ How many attendees do you expect will attend?

◆ Who is your target audience?

◆ Who else will be speaking at the event?

Every answer should be the right fit for you and your expertise. For example, if the host has not hosted many events, you will want to ask for speaker referrals to check him out in advance. Make sure the audience size and the target market are a perfect fit, and also ask who else will be presenting at the event so you eliminate the possibility of competition on your topic. The last thing you want to do is to show up at an event and find out there are two other speakers who are presenting on the same topic. That's as much a nightmare as showing up wearing the same dress! Okay, maybe this doesn't apply to the guys. But even when you do your homework in advance of signing a speaker agreement, you can still get burned. You want to at least try to avoid any possible nightmares. When you do your homework in advance, it usually sets you up for success, but that's not *always* the case...

Lessons Learned the Hard Way

Okay, now I'm going to dish on the ugly side of the event business so that you can get an idea of what to watch out for and hopefully avoid. Here are a few bad experiences I've had with hosts that went terribly wrong. I won't mention these hosts by name, but I will mention them by experience.

First there was **The Hostage Holder**. This host held the speakers captive for the entire weekend by not telling them when they would be going on stage to speak. He did this just to keep the speakers available for the full event. Usually I'll stay for the majority of an event anyway, but I don't want to be *forced* to stay. The more he tried to keep control of everything and everyone, the more he lost control. He didn't even have control of the event in the planning stages, because he filled the room with the wrong audience.

While doing my homework in advance of agreeing to speak, the host assured me that he was going to fill the event with business owners and entrepreneurs, yet the audience was much different. It turned out that 95 percent of the audience were cubicle workers from a high-tech company. They didn't want to have their own business and they didn't want to become entrepreneurs. This was not a good fit!

The host set everyone up for a disaster. The speakers couldn't sell and the audience was beaten up with high-pitch offers for days that they didn't want to invest in. The audience and the speakers were all being held hostage! When I finally got to speak on the third day of the event, I was not about to try and sell this audience. My presentation went from a sales mode to a motivational talk. At least I was able to support the audience with what they wanted and needed to hear.

Lessons Learned: No matter what happens at an event, keep your cool and remain professional. Your job is to support the host and the audience to the best of your ability. It's a small world in the expert business, and the word gets out quickly. Therefore, your reputation is more valuable than just about any other asset you possess. Every time you speak, you have the privilege of the platform and the opportunity to touch someone deeply with your message and your expertise.

Then there was **Mr. Big Shot**, who hosted a huge event in Texas. He rented out an entire convention center for a women's conference and told the speakers there would be 3,000 people attending. Some of the biggest names in the speaking business where invited to present. I was honored to be included as a headline speaker, and it was definitely a good prospective market match for my expertise. Months in advance, speakers prepared for the big event; some even flew in their entire team for sales support. I arrived a couple of days in advance to get prepared, but when I got there something didn't feel right. I did a trial run of the convention center the day before, and no one was there. Nothing and no one seemed to be prepared for the big day.

When I arrived the next morning, the convention center was still empty. Speakers were showing up and setting up their expo booths, but the audience wasn't showing up yet. After setting up my expo table, I took time to chat up my speaker friends, and as the clock ticked away we started to get nervous. It was now 8:30 a.m., and still very few attendees had arrived in the building. The event was due to kick off at 9 a.m. Yikes!

Well, you guessed it: the event was a huge NO SHOW. I got on the main stage set for 3,000 attendees at 10:30 a.m. with only 15 attendees in my audience—and most of them were my speaker friends. I've never seen an event disaster of this magnitude in my life. This one goes down in history.

Lessons Learned: I do believe that there is a reason why something happens, especially in the most challenging situations. This one was not easy to figure out at first, but here's my take on it: As a host, don't allow your ego to get in the way of making good business decisions when planning your own event. Don't expect your speakers to put butts in the seats for you. And don't focus on marketing the speakers rather than the benefits the audience will receive. Of course, Mr. Big Shot would not agree with me on these lessons, because he refused to take responsibility for his mistakes.

No one was a winner here: not the host, not the speakers, and certainly not the audience (because they didn't show up).

You get the idea of what could go wrong at events, yet most of the time the event hosts do what they say they are going to do, and it makes for a great win/win. One thing I know for sure is that each event has a life of its own, no matter who's doing the hosting.

CHAPTER 21

START YOUR OWN BIG-MONEY EVENTS

CREATING YOUR OWN EVENTS IS A GREAT WAY TO bring in a lot of income fast. Imagine hosting your own event that brings in six to seven figures and fills your coaching programs and product sales with a year's worth of income in just one weekend—every time you roll one out. Beginning to host your own events can be the turning point for dramatically increasing your expert income. This certainly was the case for me: at my own events I've created as much as $100,000 in 90 minutes on stage, and up to half a million at a three-day event. Nice paycheck if you can get it, right? There are even a select few experts who have made anywhere from $3 to $6 million from a three-day event. This is incredibly impressive, but certainly not the norm. However, it does show what can be done at big-money events with the right expert and the right audience.

Hosting your own events on a grand scale is not for the faint of heart. They take a lot of work to produce, and they can be risky. I'll confess that at times my events stress me out and drive me crazy, but I still love hosting them because I enjoy the challenge and the experience it creates for the audience. Putting on a successful event is about creating an environment where people come together to learn and get out of their comfort zones for a short period of time to create fast personal and professional growth. That's exciting! Attendees from my events will have memories they can keep for a lifetime. There is nothing quite like a live event experience.

But to create an experience, you must create more than just a learning environment. An exciting experience will have people talking about your events. For example, my events are not only educational, they are action-packed, full of surprises, and lots of fun! We laugh, we dance, we cry, we make amazing connections, and we learn. I love hearing stories from people who have dramatically changed their lives by attending my events. Now that's what I call exciting and rewarding! This is what keeps me motivated for my next event.

Imagine having the same opportunity to change someone's life at your own event. You don't have to host large events to make a difference; you just need to get started—even if it's just 10 to 20 people in a room.

So, how do you get started?

I suggest you begin with a one-day seminar and eventually work your way up to a three-day retreat, conference, summit, or workshop once your list and following grows. One of the hardest things to do in the event business is fill seats—and with the *right* people. Hosting your own event is one of the best ways to make a name for yourself in the expert business. When you host your own event, you take on all the risk, but you also get to keep all the rewards that go along with it. This also means keeping *all* of your own sales!

Hosting your own events is like prospecting on steroids. You don't have to sell yourself, because you are the main attraction! People come to your events to hear your expertise; you've already built trust with your audience and prospects before you even take the stage—even if that stage is in front of 15 people in the basement of a cheap hotel. You've got to start somewhere!

Be Prepared Before You Leap

Typically your sales will be much higher at your own events because the audience is showing up to hear *you*. But I don't suggest you launch your event business until you have been trained by another expert who has already created the success you desire. Selling from the stage is another skill set you must acquire before taking the leap into the event business; don't jump in blindly. The skill of running your own successful events and selling from the stage will dramatically cut your learning curve and increase your sales fast, and there is definitely a formula to doing it the right way. Being invested in this knowledge in advance will instantly improve your opportunities for big-money events.

With these skills in place, you can typically plan to close a good percentage of the room. Of course, this depends on who's in your audience and what your offer is. So let's say you have the right audience—great potential buyers who are hungry for your expertise. Your offer still has to be the perfect fit to help them overcome their obstacles, relieve their pain, and solve their problems. Your offer must be the answer they have been looking for.

If your audience and your offer are right, you are going to sell.

Know the What, Why, Who, and How of Your Event

What is your *why*?

You must know why you want to host your own event and what type of end results you would like to achieve before you get started. Of course, money is always the main driving factor for a highly paid expert. But what else drives you to succeed? Knowing what personally drives you to action is what will keep you going when the going gets tough.

What makes your event unique?

Know how you plan to stand out from other experts and other events in your niche market. Clearly define what type of training and experience you will create, and design an event that will make attendees talk about you and your events for years to come. Your stage, music, guest speakers— all the highlights of your event will create a unique experience. Make a difference by making memories your guests can take with them for a lifetime.

Who is your ideal target market?

Knowing whom to target and how to market to them is critical to getting the right people at your events. Every word of your marketing and every video must connect and relate to this market. Get into the minds and the hearts of your prospects even before they show up.

How will you connect your Why with your What and your Who?

When putting on an event in which you are selling a program, you must keep your closing offer in mind before you develop your training. You must understand how your training will best showcase your expertise in a way that makes prospects take action on the spot. Remember that your main goal is to sell!

Working Out the Details and Developing a System

Typically I like a long lead time of four to six months to plan a three-day event. However, in some cases I've had as little as one month to plan a repeat event if the Website was already up and ready to go. I typically don't like to rush the marketing plan. A much longer lead time removes the stress of getting everything done and filling the seats. Visualize your success outcome, stay on course, and never cancel an event because you couldn't fill seats. The only reason you can't fill seats is because you gave up too soon.

The more time you give yourself to plan an event, the more time you'll have to market and promote the event. Keep in mind that there is a lot of pre-event work to do. You'll need to get your location, negotiate the contract, set up a Website, create an e-mail and video marketing campaign, develop a social media strategy, and more—all this before you can even begin to market. This all takes time to do it right, and you can't rush the system.

Create a detailed "To-Do" check list for your event well in advance. As you complete each event, go back and revise your checklist to make it easy to follow the next time around. Developing a step-by-step system will help to make your next event run a lot smoother. Keep learning and improving as you grow and expand.

The first thing you need to do is set the date(s). Once you have a date in mind, you are then committed to take action. Consider adding a countdown clock to your event Website. You'll be amazed at how quickly your event kick-off day comes around. To get a free downloadable clock go to CountDownTo.com.

Next find your event location. If possible, always do a live site inspection to see the meeting room space, hotel lobby, restaurants, and sleeping rooms. Get a feel for what your attendees will experience when they arrive.

Go through every detail of the event with the hotel sales and catering team in advance of signing your contract. Negotiate the contract with them to get the best hotel room rates and audio/video needs. Often you can negotiate great rates at high-end resorts during their slower seasons. The hotel will also waive the cost of your meeting room space if you are providing enough meals and/or fill enough hotel rooms. Always keep your minimum hotel room block at as low a rate as possible while still getting your meeting room space waived. It takes some insight and negotiating skills to pull this off. Keep in mind that where hotels make their money is by filling hotel rooms first and selling food second, not in the meeting room space. This will help you to understand where they can negotiate.

If you aren't good at negotiating, plan to hire a meeting planner who can negotiate these things on your behalf. You certainly don't want to get stuck paying for a lot of extra hotel rooms out of your own pocket. Another thing to ask for is a free hotel room for yourself and/or your staff, or an upgrade to a suite at no additional charge;

I always get amazing upgrades to luxurious suites. Often I use my suite to host "client only" receptions, host meetings with my staff, or have private group consultations. Also keep your food and beverage to a minimum. The cost of food and coffee alone can kill your profits! For example, to cover your minimum food and beverage costs at a three-day event, you can host a VIP reception one evening of the event that would typically cost you less than offering lunches each day. For a one-day event, you may want to do lunches for VIP guests only who have paid a higher

ticket price to attend. This helps you to reach your negotiated minimums, and it adds more value for attendees.

There are so many details I can share with you on how
to host a successful event. I've learned a ton from hosting events for more than 10 years, and I'm still learning. I
could write another book on how to host your own events,
but for now, this is enough to get you started. Instead, let's
talk about money.

Show Me the Money

Typically the price point offer(s) that you present at
your own event would be higher than what you would offer
at someone else's event. The reason for this is that you already have warm prospects that know and trust you. They
are more likely to invest in your higher-end programs, especially if your event runs for three days. This is *not* the
place to sell your $20 book at the back of the room!

You don't need a huge audience to be successful at
events. By offering high-end programs, you don't have
to sell a lot of people to make a lot of money. You also
don't need to sell a huge percentage of the room to walk
away with a big paycheck. For example, I hosted an
event at a very exclusive resort in Sedona, Arizona. The
Enchantment Resort and Spa is an amazing place, sur-
rounded by a stunning red rock canyon; it's truly a magical
place. I decided to host my event at this location because
I had always wanted the opportunity to stay there in one
of their amazing suites. I figured if *I* wanted to stay there,

so would my attendees, and only the people who could afford it would show up. Just 35 attendees paid to attend this weekend marketing retreat. The audience wasn't large, but they were the right prospects; they were serious about their business. In fact, one attendee flew all the way from New Zealand to be there.

At the end of three magical days in Sedona, I had sold just a handful of new clients. Out of the 35 that attended, I sold seven attendees with an offer of $17,997. Therefore, I had sold 20 percent of the room and walked away with a paycheck of $125,979. Not a shabby paycheck for such a small group, especially when this was the first event at which I had ever tried to sell a high-end consulting package. The reason I share this story with you is to let you know that you don't have to pack a room to make big money from events. You should also never underestimate what someone would pay to invest in your expertise when you offer great value.

When you host your own events, you take on all the risk, but you also get to keep all of the sales. You can easily sell a high-end program with a one-day event, but you'll usually sell more when you host a three-day event. Start out with a one-day and work your way up to a three-day event. Now you might be thinking, *Why not do a two-day event?* That's because there is an energy flow around a three-day event that works even better. Three days allow you more time to bring in guest speakers and have more interaction with the audience. The more time attendees spend with you and the more value you give them through education, the more they will trust you and buy from you.

Therefore, three-day events give you the opportunity to sell even higher priced packages.

Avoid Being Spanked for Making Too Much Money

The first year I started to host events, I did small, local, one-day business seminars that held 30 to 50 people. This helped me to quickly become known as a local marketing expert. I had no idea how to sell from the stage yet, but I made money from ticket sales and gained a few new clients. The next year, I decided to go big-time by launching my first three-day event. I had no idea the magnitude of what was about to develop. I just jumped in with both feet. It was a huge risk, but I wanted to make my mark in the event business. Call me crazy—and even more clueless! But luckily the event sold out with a large crowd of 600 attendees. This was not an easy task, especially for a woman, as most big events were hosted by men at that time.

I remember how exciting it was seeing people flowing into the ballroom as I got ready to take the stage to kick off the event on day one. The first day flowed nicely without too much drama...except for the fact that we had no sales. This started stressing me out, because I had invested a ton of money in this event. I thought, *Yikes, if we don't sell at this event, it could end up taking me years to pay it off.*

On day two, the event took a turn, and sales started flowing in. Attendees started investing so quickly that we didn't know how to keep up with the credit card sales.

Really, I have to confess that both my team and I were flying by the seat of our pants, in unchartered territory. It was like watching a duck above water: smooth sailing on the top, but underneath we were paddling as fast as we could to keep up. By the end of third day we had generated more than a million dollars in sales. Wow! How easy was that?—or so I thought. I was soon to learn another hard lesson in the event business that would cost me dearly.

About a week after the event, I got a call from my merchant account company telling me it was urgent they speak to me right away. They told me that they would need to hold the sales from credit cards for four to six weeks before releasing the funds to my bank. That was the majority of my sales! I had maxed out my own credit cards to make this event happen, and now I had bills to pay with no income. It was a stressful time trying to get it worked out with the merchant account company. After holding it together for about a month, they called me again and said they needed to hold my funds for *another* six months, and that my merchant account had been frozen.

This was probably the most stressful time I've ever had in business; an experience I would not want to relive again. What I was soon to discover (far too late) was that I had exceeded my normal sales volume with the merchant account company due to the huge spike in my sales. When this happens, merchant account companies can hold your funds for an extended period of time to review the charges for any possible fraud.

Luckily I found a new merchant account company that agreed to take me on right away and run the charges, and my sales were saved. Don't make this same mistake! To avoid this, you must communicate with your merchant account company well in advance of your event to tell them there will be a spike in your regular sales volumes. It's all about learning and communication. Basically, if you don't set up your sales parameters correctly in advance of a big income-generating event, you could get spanked pretty hard for not having your average sales thresholds increased.

Putting on big events is not for the faint-of-heart. You must be somewhat of a risk-taker to launch an event of this magnitude, yet anyone can host smaller events and work their way up to a size that feels comfortable for them. Either way, events can be one of the most profitable and fast ways to grow your expert income.

CHAPTER 22

GENERATE MULTIPLE STREAMS OF EXPERT INCOME

EVERYTHING YOU'VE LEARNED IN THIS BOOK UP to this point has been to help you build a very successful expert business that you can monetize. But now it's time to take a look at your money goals and how you can develop consistent streams of income. The ultimate goal of your business should be to generate consistent income and get paid what you're worth. So what does "highly paid" mean for you? What are your ultimate income goals? Would you be happy making $100,000 a year? Or is your goal to make $500,000, $1 million, or even millions each year?

Your income goal should be a bit of a stretch, but you should also be realistic about what is possible based upon your current situation. It's easy to say, "I want to make a million dollars." That's a nice round number that a lot of people wish to achieve. However, if you are just starting out in business with little experience behind you, making a million your first year is highly unlikely.

What It Takes to Become a Millionaire

You often hear about experts who teach people to become millionaires practically overnight. That's a hard promise to deliver! Unless that expert plans to live with you, invest with you, and give you their absolutely no-fail, step-by-step system, it's not likely to happen. If it was that easy to become a millionaire, there would be a lot more wealthy people on the planet.

Becoming a millionaire from your own expertise takes time and a high level of commitment to achieve. There are a lot of factors that come into play in becoming a millionaire. Millionaires have traits and skills that most other people don't possess; they think and act differently. They have the right mindset, a high level of focus, and determination to achieve their goals. They are more willing and more open to taking risks. They also understand how to develop successful strategies to grow their businesses. And one important thing that the majority of them have in common is that they know how to develop multiple streams of income. Millionaires rarely have just one stream of income.

Did you realize that to become a millionaire you'll need to generate an average of $83,000 per month, for one full year? That's a lot of money. So you'll need some streams of income that don't require much of your personal time so that you can work on growing your business. This is called passive income.

You may already be a millionaire and you're working to grow your business to an even higher level. If so, good for you. I understand the level of commitment it takes to get there. Your first million is usually the hardest to achieve. Once you've reached this high level of success, you most likely have reached the top of your niche market and have achieved a certain level of celebrity status from your expertise and experience. You would also have a team and systems in place that allow your business to continue to grow with ease. However, if your income level is nowhere near millionaire status just yet, it's going to take some time and a lot of focus to get there. One way to move you up the income ladder faster is to develop multiple streams of income that flow to you on a consistent basis.

Set Realistic Goals as You Grow Your Business

Few people take the time to look at the real numbers when it comes to setting income goals, so they set lofty goals that set them up for failure. If you are just starting out as an expert, a realistic goal for you to shoot for may be $100,000 per year. This can become a reality if you already have a quality brand, an effective marketing plan, and some high-level clients in place. To make $100,000 a year, you will need to generate an average of $8,300 per month. (This means your gross income, excluding taxes, business expenses, and so on.)

You may need to reconsider your ultimate income goal target. Whatever that number is, you need to have a goal that is a bit of a stretch to achieve, but one that's not too challenging. You want to set yourself up for success to achieve and/or even exceed your goals.

5 Ways to Grow Multiple Streams of Income

1. **Manifest and multiply only your most ideal clients.** Your marketing must be on target and directed only towards your most ideal prospects. Ensure that each client you take on is a good fit for your programs. If he is not the right fit, it will only cause you more work and headaches in the long run. If you believe that a prospect is not the right fit, be honest with him up front. You can say no and still remain professional and fair. If you are doing personal coaching or consulting, you only want clients who can afford your fees and those who appreciate the high-quality expertise and service you have to offer. And if you are hiring other coaches, they must be the perfect fit to allow your company to grow.

2. **Develop joint venture affiliates who can sell your products.** Develop joint venture partnerships and affiliate programs so that others

can help you promote and sell your products. You can also make affiliate income from their product sales in return. Affiliates can become another income stream whereby you promote someone else's products, events, and so on, and get paid a percentage for the sales you generate. Most affiliate programs are done via e-mail or social media connections.

3. **Generate big-income days.** Events will help you gain instant clients in one day. Focus on selling your high-end programs at these events. Set up your own live events or workshops. An event can be an evening seminar, full-day to multiple-day workshops, or even an online course.

4. **Create high-level coaching or consulting programs.** Support people one on one (or in small groups) in a specific niche or industry. Share your wisdom and expertise to show others how to improve either their businesses or personal lives. You can also add additional coaches to your team to expand your reach.

5. **Develop a license or franchise business model with your expertise.** Set up a systemized program you can sell to others. This could include licensing or franchising your existing expert model of training, or by expanding a coaching business with additional coaches. If you can sell your training programs from a licensing deal, it can become very profitable.

Develop Your Multiple-Streams-of-Income Plan

Consider what streams of income would best work for your expertise. As you develop these different streams of income, consider how much annual income you plan to generate from each stream. Also consider what percentage of income each stream would generate. Keep in mind how much personal time each product or service would require from you and how quickly you can generate income from each project. Here is a list of income-generating offers to consider:

Personal coaching, consulting, or mentoring.

Group coaching programs.

Mastermind programs.

VIP days: live and virtual.

Client-only retreats.

Online classes: teleseminars or Webinars.

Online courses or certifications.

Video training.

◆ Google Hangout series.

Live stream programs.

Product sales: CDs, DVDs, downloads, etc.

Workbooks.

Books and e-books.

Membership program.

Paid professional speaking.

◆ Emcee or expert panel.

- Affiliate income.

- Joint venture partnerships.

- Branded products: t-shirts, mugs, etc.

- Sales income from other speakers.

- Ticket sales from events.

Now let's put together a plan for your multiple streams of income. Grab a large piece of paper to get started. In the center of the paper, put one large circle. Inside the circle, write in your annual income goal. Now draw additional circles around the main circle for all the income-generating streams you plan to create. Next, write all the streams of income in the smaller circles. Go around the page until you have all the circles filled in using items from the list I provided. Use the following diagram as your guide.

MULTIPLE STREAMS OF INCOME

Annual Income — Coaching Consulting, Tele-Class Webinars, Online Courses, Product Sales, Book Sales, Affiliate Income, Paid Speaking, Live Events, VIP Days

Once you have created your income streams, you'll need to think about what percentage of income each stream will generate. Calculate percentages for each stream of income. This will give you a strong visual of what areas you need to focus on the most and what areas of income will become more passive. Once your streams of income are broken down, you'll be able to see how much income you'll need to generate from each stream.

Let's use $100,000 annual income as an example. If you want to generate 50 percent of your income from coaching or consulting, you'll need to make $50,000 per year from this one stream. If your clients pay you an average of $3,000 for your services, you'll need to take on 17 personal clients per year to achieve your goal for this area of income. Experts can easily generate the largest percentage of their income from personal one-on-one time. Now consider your clients paying you an average of $5,000; you would then only need to take on 10 personal clients at this rate to reach your income goal for this stream.

Breaking down your income streams and having a goal written down for each area will allow you to easily create a workable action plan that makes sense for your business. Focus first on the areas that can generate the most income. As your business and fees increase, you can decide to either take on more clients or add another stream of income to increase your annual revenues. Do the math ahead of time with your percentage breakdowns so you won't get stuck wondering why you didn't achieve your ultimate income goal.

As your business grows and shifts, you can make adjustments to your income streams, along with the percentages and income from each one. You'll also discover new areas of your business that can generate good income, but require little of your personal time. These may be areas you'll want to expand as your business grows.

You will achieve what you focus on the most!

CHAPTER 23

GET YOUR "ASK" IN GEAR

WE'VE SPENT A LOT OF TIME DISCUSSING MONEY, and for good reason: if you don't know how to ask for, or how to make and manage large sums of money, you're not going to make it to the highly paid expert level at the top of the pyramid (as referenced in Chapter 5). Your income can grow only to the extent that you do.

Not knowing how to *ask* stops the flow of opportunities and money. There are a lot of people who are uncomfortable asking for money. If asking for money doesn't come easy, you must learn how to ramp up your courage to ask for—and get—what you're worth.

Limiting beliefs around money keeps it from flowing to you.

5 Fast Ways to Get Your "Ask" in Gear

1. **Get clear on what you want.** Start by asking yourself, *Exactly what is it that I need to receive from this person to assist me in achieving my short-term goals?* For example, *I want to ask this person to co-host an event, become an affiliate partner, promote my book,* or *buy my services.*

2. **Understand what you're really worth, and why.** Break down the long-term value that you bring to clients and think about the results you generate for your most valued clients. What is your experience, your knowledge, and your guidance really worth? Your expertise could make a profound impact on someone's life—that's priceless!

3. **Identify what you are actually afraid of.** Is facing rejection what you're afraid of? Rejection doesn't make you a failure, but failing to learn from it most certainly will. The best way to get over the fear of rejection is to face it head-on. As with all fears, once you've confronted it a few times, it will start to lose its power over you.

We all get rejected from time to time—it's just a part of doing business.

4. **Practice asking.** Many people are afraid to ask for what they want. So they go without. If you don't ask, you don't get! Get in the habit of asking for something every day (even if it's small), and you'll be surprised how much more you receive. Do this every day for three weeks and you'll see your fears about asking diminish significantly.

5. **Gain rave reviews and testimonials from your clients.** When you have a client who has received great value from working with you, ask her for a testimonial. Ask her what her return was from investing in your product or services. Great testimonials that showcase income-generating results will easily justify your high-priced expert fees. It doesn't matter what you pay for something as long as your return is greater.

Act in Spite of Discomfort

The majority of us are creatures of habit, especially when habits have been programed into our brains for years. In fact, some of us are so conditioned against asking that we are completely closed-minded to it.

About 95 percent of what we think and do is habitual. It takes time to form new beliefs and to act upon new habits. Programming and conditioning in our past does not necessarily serve us well today or in the future. Every be-lief we have will either move us forward or keep us stuck in the same place. Beliefs and thoughts can empower us or disempower us. Thoughts and beliefs are not real unless we give them power.

Once we know better, we do better. Consciousness is observing our thoughts and actions so that we can live from true choices in the present moment, rather than from our past programming.

If you are going to give your thoughts and beliefs power, why not empower yourself with only positive beliefs that support your success at a much higher level? Having the ability to ask for what you want brings the world to your doorstep. Some people are excellent at asking for and getting what they want because they believe they can. Others see these people as extremely lucky. However, luck has very little to do with knowing what you want, and ev-erything to do with asking for it in the proper way.

You must be willing to ask for what you want, be it asking a prospect to buy from you, asking a client to give you a referral, or asking someone to bring you in to speak to his organization. Whatever it is you want, start by ask-ing with the belief and expectation that you will receive it. Never stop asking!

To receive something that you want, you have to ask for it. Period! The power is in the asking and in the expectation that you will receive it.

CHAPTER 24

BECOME THE AUTHORITY BY WRITING A BOOK

"REPUTATION" AND "VISIBILITY" ARE THE TOP TWO reasons buyers invest in books. Therefore, writing your own book brings a higher level of credibility to your expertise, and being a successful author builds your value. Yet does the book itself make you money as a highly paid expert? The book itself is not necessarily going to get you rich; it's the opportunities that a book creates that are where most of the income-generating possibilities will come from.

People often ask me this question: "How do you write a book?" A small percentage of people who ask this question hope to hear, "Anyone can write a book." Most just want permission. But the truth is they don't need permission and there are no rules to book writing; there is no license required and no test to take. Writing requires no financial resources—just a writing tool and paper (or a computer) and some focused effort are all that has been required for hundreds of years. If the Marquis de Sade could write a book in prison using a quill (or anything else he could get his hands on), you can certainly write a book from the comfort of your own home. How do you write a book? "Butt in the chair!" Just sit down and write! What it takes is an extended commitment of time. That's why few aspiring authors actually end up getting their work published.

After I completed my first book, I thought, *I'll never write another book because it's too much work*—and now this is my sixth book. Never say never! Writing a book is not only time consuming, but it's actually somewhat of a self-indulgent process with lots of focused alone time. The upside to taking the time to write is the final outcome: you're a published author!

What I really enjoy about books is the notion that people can make up creative thoughts in their minds and then turn it into something real on paper. Words can be powerful. I love seeing books come to life. It inspires me to keep going. There is nothing like holding your new baby (your book) in your hands once you've given birth to it, so to speak. As a published author, you also learn to love and respect books even more. If you like being creative and turning words into sentences, then you might just learn to love the process of writing too!

Your Book Will Open Many Doors

Your book is probably not going to make you a famously rich rock-star bestselling author; writing is not the way that most experts get rich. Instead look at your book as a door-opening opportunity that supports your highly paid expert business. It can be an amazing marketing tool to sell your expertise.

More than 100,000 thousand books are published in the United States alone every year, and few sell more than a few thousand copies. But that's not going to stop you from writing a book. As an expert, it's the best way to increase your income from the spin-offs the book can create: products, speaking, coaching, events, and even movie opportunities can come from your book. For example, it was my book that got me into the motivational movie *The Compass*. The movie's producer, John Spencer Ellis, had found my book in a bookstore and asked me, along with many other experts I featured in my book, to be in the movie. Within a matter of days from our very first phone call, Ellis had a camera crew fly to Phoenix to shoot my part in the movie—all from the exposure that my book created. You never know who's going to pick up your book and ask for your support as an expert.

It doesn't take magic to write a book, it's just a bunch of words. Nothing is stopping you from collecting information, coming up with a title, and getting started right now. Writing a good book, compared to a bad one, involves one thing: work! You can call it effort, study, practice, or whatever. Sure, there are tricks here and there, but writing is really a commitment of work. Yet once you get a system in place for getting your book done, it becomes easier. For example, it took me just three months to write this book—that was a record-breaking time for me, especially with all the other business commitments and a heavy workload already on my plate.

Develop a System to Get Your Book Written Quickly

There is no such thing as writer's block! The only reason you should get stuck writing your book is not knowing which direction to go. A system, plan, or layout will help you to visualize and gain focus so that you have a clear direction. So before you start writing, create your book layout by doing a brainstorming session. I call this my Brand-Storm Book-Writing System.

Let's try out the first part of this system right now. You'll need a very large piece of paper, a poster, or a flip chart to make this work. Begin by drawing one large circle in the middle of the page. This is where you will write the title of your book. Leave plenty of room around the big circle to add more. Next, create one longer circle right below the large circle. This is where your subtitle will go. Next add 10 smaller circles around the outside of the large circle and the one below it. This is where you will add your chapter titles. Below the chapter title circles, add additional circles for the sub-chapters. Use the following diagram as your guide.

BRAND-STORM BOOK OUTLINE

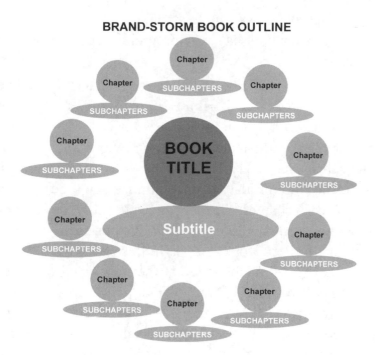

Your title is extremely important. It is part of the overall impression you're creating about your book. Your book title will set a tone and create a promise for the book to deliver. But don't get hung up on trying to figure out the perfect title just yet—that's what your Brand-Storming session is for. Your subtitle should be a strong, benefit-rich statement that describes what the reader will learn from your book. For example, the subtitle of this book is, "Turn Your Passion, Skills, and Talents into a Lucrative Career by Becoming the Go-To Authority in Your Industry." In each of the other smaller circles all around the one main circle, write out your chapter titles. You'll need to Brand-Storm these chapter ideas as you go along. Create at least 10 circles, or 10 chapters, that work around the concept of your title and subtitle.

As you see your title, subtitle, and chapter titles come together, keep Brand-Storming to add more. You'll want to come up with sub-heading ideas for each one of your chapter titles. Add smaller circles below each chapter for your subchapter titles. To come up with good headings, you'll want to consider all of the things you'll be writing about in each chapter. This allows you to chunk down your book into topics and ideas so that it's not such an overwhelming project. For example, in this chapter, "Become the Authority by Writing a Book," there are heading topics: "Your Book Will Open Many Doors," "Develop a System to Get Your Book Written Quickly," and so on. Each chapter is broken down into chunks of information or ideas. Keep brainstorming until you have filled out the entire page. You'll begin to see how the title, subtitle, chapters, and chapter headings all start coming together to create an overall flow for your book.

If you aren't good at coming up with catchy titles and putting together a step-by-step marketing plan for your book, you may want to consider working with an expert who can help you get it done fast. For example, my clients will use my virtual VIP days to get a project like this knocked out in half a day, plus a marketing plan for their book. Once your Brand-Storm Book-Writing System is in place you should be able to easily start writing the book section by section. Of course you'll need to tweak and adjust your chapter titles and heading titles as you go, but it's a great jumpstart to the overall book-writing process.

Your Brand-Storm Book-Writing System should include:

◆ A working book title.

◆ A benefit-rich subtitle that tells what the book is about.

◆ Chapter titles and heading title ideas.

◆ A rough draft or overview of the entire book.

◆ A detailed layout completed before first book draft.

◆ Notes from your chapter ideas and research.

◆ A marketing plan to get the word out about the book well in advance of completion.

Your Book Will Be Judged at First Glance

They say that people judge a book by its cover; they also judge a book by its subtitle, chapter titles, and overall layout. Most people will look at the front cover, back cover, and chapter titles before deciding if they want to buy the book or not. That's why it's so important to create titles that jump off the page and make the viewer want to buy your book.

Once you have completed your brand-storming session, it should motivate you to start writing, because you'll see the whole concept of your book. Start chunking the book down even more. Make notes, do research, and write down ideas for each chapter until you've created a rough draft for the book. If your book flows well and navigates the reader through a process, it will also take your readers on a journey. If you've done a great job, your readers will want to take action to purchase more products from you, attend an event, and/or hire you as a coach or mentor. Remember, your book is a great marketing tool to promote your expertise and your services.

Don't Bother Writing a Book Unless You Plan to Market It

As an expert, I believe that you should always make the commitment to write your book, but only when the timing is right for you. You need time to not only write the book, but to market it too. Marketing should happen very early on in the writing stage, not after the book is completed!

If you are still in the process of growing your expert business, it's not time for you to write a book quite yet—go out and get some clients and make some money first. It always shocks me when I hear someone say they are taking off work for one to two years to write their book. Now that's absolutely crazy! And what's even crazier is that most of them have no idea how to market the book once it's completed and have no database to market it to. If they had any idea of what they were doing, they could have knocked that book out with a marketing plan in place in a matter of months—even working on it part time.

Marketing is where you should put your efforts as you write the book. Your marketing plan should include both offline and online promotion. You'll need strong joint venture partners in place to help you market and sell your book when it launches. Well in advance of your book's completion, it should have its own well-crafted Website.

Writing your book will certainly expand your level of expertise and allow you to be seen as an authority on your chosen topic. But keep in mind that your book is going to basically be a marketing tool that helps you gain more business. Writing your book is just the beginning; it's the marketing that makes it sell. The most successful best-selling books got there because they had a great marketing plan in place.

> *The most important part of writing a book is*
> *MARKETING a book!*

A great example of how important marketing can be is the best-selling book *Everything Men Know About Women*. This book is *completely empty* inside. There are no words on the pages. This book has been successfully marketed and sold since 1985. The marketing campaign is what made this empty book a bestseller. If that doesn't convince you how important marketing your book is, then I'm not sure what will.

A successful marketing plan is what separates successful authors from authors who sell only a few hundred books. Why take all the time to do the work for a few hundred book sales? It's not worth it! And even if you do find a major publisher for your book, they are not going to be the main source of your marketing. They have lots of books to market. *You* will always be the one who's responsible to promote, market, and sell your books!

Should You Self-Publish or Get a Major Publisher?

Publishers are justifiably picky because they get pitched thousands of books a day. It takes effort to learn the ropes, send out brilliant book queries, and do the research required to craft the idea for a book and then propose it effectively. Finding a publisher is no mystery, but getting them to accept your proposal is another thing altogether. It's not likely a major publisher will pick up your book if you are a first-time author. However, if you are already a highly successful expert with a good marketing plan, a full speaking schedule, and media engagements lined up, you just might get picked up.

I got lucky securing my New York book agent, Jessica Faust of BookEnds. She found me from a Google search; few authors get a book agent this way, but experts who already have a great online presence have a good shot at it. Jessica has sold three books of mine to three different publishers. When Jessica sent the proposal out for this book, I had a number of major publishers respond immediately with their interest. My agent negotiated with publishers back and forth for a couple of months before deciding on Career Press. I choose this publisher because they gave me the shortest deadline for publication. I wanted to get the book out there fast. Nothing will motivate you more to complete your book than a signed contract with a check waiting for you on the other side!

If you don't get picked up by a major publisher, self-publishing is the way to go. The good news is that it's a lot easier today to self-publish than ever before. If you want to get your book out there fast and make a name for yourself, self-publishing is a great way to go. With self-publishing, you have total control over your title, content, cover, and sales. Yet you also need to do all the work to get it published. That's the reason they call it self-publishing. Today, self-publishing can be easier than you think. You can become your own publisher at any time and print any number of books you wish. Print on Demand (POD) costs are now low, making it easy to print a short run of books. With POD, there is no inventory piled up in your garage, because you are able to print any number of books you need with a quick turnaround time.

You'll need to hire an editor and a book designer, but otherwise the base costs can be minimal to get your book out there. As an expert, you should have lots of great information to share, so writing a book should not be a challenge for you. Getting it done and meeting a deadline, however, might be. As a self-published author, you need to create your own deadline, and you need to stick to it. If you are not good at staying focused and keeping deadlines, you may want to consider hiring a book coach. A good book coach can help by walking you through the step-by-step process of getting published. He will also help to cut your learning curve on the writing process, build your confidence, keep you motivated, and keep you on track of reaching your publication goal. One of my clients, Shelley Gillespie, is an expert book-writing coach who can help you meet your deadlines and get your book completed on time. Learn more about her services at BookWritingSuccessCoach.com.

One very important thing I suggest as a self-published author is to have a professional cover created. People do judge a book by its cover! If it doesn't look great on the outside, it's probably not going to sell. It's worth the investment to get it done right. You want to feel proud of and excited about your book. So don't go cheap on your book cover! For a professional book cover design similar to what you would see from a major publisher, expect to pay anywhere from $500 to $1,500.

Going From Clueless to Best-Seller

If I can do it, so can you! I had no idea that I could ever become a successful author. I still remember something my English teacher once said to me: "If you don't pass this next test, you're going to flunk out of high school." When I wrote my first book, this message was still stuck in my head; I believed that because I wasn't good in English, I wouldn't be a good writer. That's why I decided to write my first book interview-style. By adding other experts to my book, I felt more confident about publishing a book that I could put my name on. My first book was a small 100-page niche book for retailers called *Trade Secrets of Retail Stars*. I enjoyed the interviews and creative process of putting the book together, but when it was completed, I remember being so clueless that I didn't even know how to download the file onto a floppy disc (I'm dating myself here). So I took my entire computer to a professional printer, and asked them to copy it and print the book. Yes, clueless for sure!

Back then, short-run printing was not available, so I asked my local printer to print 1,500 copies. My speaking career was just beginning; I had no clue how to market the book and had no joint venture partners to help me sell books. And if someone asked me what Amazon was, I would have said "It's a jungle!"

But I was an author! A newly published author, with not just one book but *1,500* books. It took me seven years to sell them all and get them out of my garage. It's amazing I ever wrote another book, right? While there was still a pile of books in my garage, I was trying to reinvent my expert business. I was going from being a retail business expert to more of a mainstream marketing expert once my second book was launched on self-promotion marketing. That book became a bestseller. And this book you are currently holding is my sixth book.

The lesson: You can go from clueless to bestseller when you learn the book-publishing business and get some great marketing behind you. Happy writing!

CHAPTER 25

DEVELOP A STEADY STREAM OF REFERRALS

REFERRALS ARE THE SUPPORT SYSTEM OF ANY business. Every expert with an endless stream of referrals has peace of mind. Wouldn't it be great if the majority of your clients came from referrals? That sure would make your job a lot easier! You are probably doing everything you can to provide excellent products and deliver the highest quality of service, and no doubt you have a great reputation as an expert and your clients already love you. If that's the case, why aren't you getting all the referrals you deserve?

The good news is that your existing clients who are pleased with their purchases and your service will automatically want to help you out with more referrals. Maybe you just need to learn the art of asking for more referrals and testimonials. Studies have proven that the one answer to why most people don't get referrals is simply that they don't ask. There are two reasons why this happens: either they forget, or they don't feel comfortable enough to ask.

The benefits from referrals are unquestionable, and the value of word-of-mouth advertising is priceless! Strive to have as much of your business as possible come from referrals because referrals are the absolute best way to attract new clients with little effort.

Referrals offer priceless opportunities because they:

◆ Open doors of opportunity that you cannot open on your own.

◆ Give you more credibility and pre-sell your expertise.

◆ Make your job easier and more enjoyable.

◆ Motivate more people to do business with you.

◆ Are more profitable than chasing after prospects who don't know you.

Referral Rewards Are a Powerful Marketing Tool

One way to kick your referral business into high gear is to offer a referral reward. Find a way to reward your customers for every referral they send you, and make sure that you systemize this process so you can test the effectiveness of your referral rewards. Be consistent so you never forget to pass along the reward that you promised your customer. The more consistent and systemized you are about asking for referrals and offering rewards, the more effective your results will be.

Learn to get comfortable asking for referrals, because they should become part of your overall business plan. Let your clients know about your referral reward program up front; getting great rewards is an added benefit of being your client. You can even plant referral reward triggers throughout your sales presentation as an additional benefit of being a client.

Another good time to ask for referrals is when your clients are raving about you, your company, your product, and/or your services. What do you say when a client gives you a compliment? Do you simply say thank you and stop at that, or do you see this as a great opportunity to ask for a referral? After you receive the compliment, continue your conversation: "Thank you very much. A wonderful testimonial like that would really help my business, and also would help a lot of other people get the same great results you did. May I ask you to refer my services to your friends and business associates?" Your client most likely will reply with an agreeable *yes* to both requests. Next, whip out your iPhone and get that testimonial on video right away!

Teach Your Clients How to Refer You

Tell your clients exactly what you would like them to do when they refer you. Don't leave it up to chance, and don't leave out any details. For example, I have two ways for my clients to easily refer people to my business. First of all, my clients receive a Website link to an online questionnaire when they sign up for my program. They can easily direct their referrals to this page via e-mail, and once their referral submits the questionnaire online, the referral gets scheduled for a free 10-minute mentoring call with me. The second way I make it easy for my clients to refer me is to pass along VIP guest tickets to attend my live Highly Paid Expert Workshop. All they have to do is pass this free gift along to their friends, family, or business associates. Clients benefit by inviting guests who will gain not only from being there, but also when guests invest in my programs.

Your referral rewards need to be generous enough to get your clients excited about referring people to your business, and they must be systemized. Remember, it's always easier to get referrals from clients who already love working with you than to try to develop new relationships on your own. The trust with a referral is already built in. The true value of one client could actually be worth many times his own value once you see the results his referrals can bring your way. Therefore, the value of one ideal client is much higher than taking on a bunch of clients who can't afford your services or don't refer you well. Great clients will send you great referrals!

Referrals Create Warm Leads

Highly paid experts have clients who come to them with ease; they don't need to chase down prospects to get them to buy. Referrals fill the pipeline and keep business flowing in. Increasing your referral business will make your job easier, your work more profitable, and your business more enjoyable.

Today's consumer is more knowledgeable, and also less trusting. Consumers want to know you, like you, and trust you. Many of them have already been burned by unethical "experts" who didn't follow through with their promises. Once trust and truth are developed in a prospect's mind, the walls come down and you can begin to quickly build an effective buyer/seller relationship. Testimonials are evidence of goodwill, and should be treated as an asset to you and your company. Don't hesitate to do whatever it takes to satisfy your clients. You will be rewarded many times over with repeat business, referrals, amazing testimonials, and powerful marketing tools that will help your expertise soar.

Network With Other Experts to Expand Your Lead Source

Brainstorming and networking with other like-minded experts is a powerful way to create more business. You can't go it alone in this competitive marketplace; you need the help and knowledge of other successful experts who can refer significant business to you. Other experts can become your greatest source of warm leads. You also need other experts' testimonials and endorsements to help you grow your business. I've always found that my competition has helped me gain a lot of business and opportunity. Sharing, supporting, and networking with other experts should be part of your overall business plan. There are opportunities everywhere for you to meet and connect with other experts. Every time you attend a conference, seminar, workshop, business function, or chamber meeting, there are opportunities to meet other experts.

By connecting with experts in complementary industries, you will gain an invaluable stream of qualified referrals and new prospective customers. Throughout the years, I've developed some amazing partnerships, friendships, and referrals from other experts whom I've met at events. This includes some of the highest-paid experts in the business—some are billionaires. They have become my friends and my mentors, and many have also become joint venture partners who have promoted my events, my books, and my expertise.

When you discover a good connection with another expert, make a point to create a memorable first impression. Instead of going up to her and telling her all about you and your expertise, begin by showing support for her business first. Make suggestions on how you may be able to work together, and send referrals from your own clients who can use her services. Be open and make it easy for her to say yes to connecting with you. When you have developed this powerful networking skill, you'll see it pay off over and over again.

Think of networking as a necessity to discovering additional contacts and referrals, and commit to making top-level networking a part of your ongoing business plan. I'm sure you're working in your own business or organization every day, and you probably find it hard to have the time to network. But when you get out and work *on* your business instead of just *in* it, you'll quickly uncover the rewards that networking at this high level has to offer.

Testimonials and Endorsements Can Rock Your World

Potential prospects may not always believe what you have to say about your products or services, and they might not believe all that your marketing has to say either. However, most *will* believe what your satisfied clients have to say about you and your organization. That is why using testimonials in all of your marketing will magnify your success rate in converting prospects into clients. Add video testimonials to your YouTube channel and your Website. Not only will video testimonials help you gain more business opportunities, but they will also help you to gain more visibility from the various search engines. Is that a win/win, or what?

When it comes to getting endorsements for your book, you'll need to get a bit shameless and write them yourself. Yes, you heard me correctly: write them yourself, and give them to your clients as examples. This doesn't mean that the person endorsing you will actually use the statement you wrote, but it will give him some ideas to follow as a guide. Most people are too busy to read your entire book before endorsing it—especially other busy experts—so you must make it easy for them to get an endorsement back to you quickly. If it's not easy, you probably won't get the referral.

If you've done well at building quality business alliances and connecting with other experts in advance of writing your book, you'll have a great lead source for joint venture partners. Joint venture partners will not only endorse your book; they can promote it for you too.

Here's how to get great endorsements fast:

Write out a detailed one-page description of your book. Think of this as a short book proposal written strictly for the benefit of gaining testimonials. In your testimonial proposal, explain what the book promises to deliver to its readers, what makes your book unique, and why you are the expert to write it.

Under your description (or proposal), list some suggested endorsements. Who knows your book better than you do, and who could write a better endorsement than you? Often your clients will pick an endorsement from your suggested list and add their own spin to it, making it even better. You just need to give them something to start with. Either way, it will allow them to take immediate action and get that great endorsement back to you fast.

For example, even before writing this book, my publisher asked me to get some endorsements for their pre-publication marketing piece. The book wasn't completed, but I needed quick endorsements based upon my reputation and experience in my industry as an expert. I put together a testimonial proposal along with some suggested endorsements, and e-mailed it to my business alliances and high-level-expert colleagues. This made it easy to get a lot of great endorsements within just a few days. In fact, within just five minutes, I had received my first endorsement from world-class marketing expert Joe Vitale. Joe is one of those high-level experts who has made millions from sharing his expertise. He is most well-known for his books and for also being featured in the movie *The Secret*. I got to know Joe first as a mentor by reading all of his marketing books, and then one day we met at a live event. The event was a premier for the movie *The Compass*, in which we were both featured. We made a great connection there and stayed in touch throughout the years. I continue to support Joe's successful best-selling book launches, and in return he supports me. This is just one example of how expert alliances can continue to refer and endorse each other at very high levels.

Asking for endorsements is a powerful way of connecting with key players in your industry. People are often flattered to be asked to endorse a book. And the people who end up endorsing the book will then have some small sense of ownership because their names are in your book and they've endorsed you. This gives you a reason to go back to them after the book is out and ask for help spreading the word. That's when their referrals will also help you sell books. And when you sell books, you sell your expertise and your services. It's all about getting the word out about your expertise and playing a much better game in business and in life.

CONCLUSION

THE TIME TO STEP UP TO A BIGGER GAME IS *NOW*!

You must be completely committed to stepping up your game. This means putting everything you've got into making it happen. Remove any limitations you may have on how much you are willing to risk and how much you are willing to sacrifice in order to exceed your goals and make it to the top.

You must be driven to succeed despite any obstacle, challenge, or setback. It doesn't matter where you are now—what matters is where you are going, and how you are getting there.

Join my expert community to receive free online training at TheHighlyPaidExpert.com.

Learn more about how to become a highly paid expert by attending my next live event at HighlyPaidExpertWorkshop. com.

INDEX

ABOUT THE AUTHOR

DEBBIE ALLEN, THE EXPERT OF EXPERTS, IS a business and brand strategist, best-selling author, and award-winning entrepreneur. Debbie has been a highly successful entrepreneur since the young age of 19, building and selling six million-dollar companies in diverse industries. Since launching her speaking and consulting business in 1995, Debbie has presented before audiences of thousands in 28 countries. She mentors clients on how to dramatically improve their marketing, brand, and overall business strategy.

After consulting and mentoring clients for nearly two decades, Debbie developed her Authority Domination Formula, which helps her clients expand their expertise, move miles past their competition, make more sales, and increase their income.

Learn more about Debbie's expertise, personalized mentoring programs, speaking presentations, and live events at DebbieAllen.com.